WORLD FAMOUS
CULTS AND FANATICS

WORLD FAMOUS
CULTS AND
FANATICS

Colin Wilson
with Damon and Rowan Wilson

SIENA

This is a Siena Book
Siena is an imprint of Parragon Book Service Ltd

Produced by Magpie Books, 1996
First published by Magpie Books, London
an imprint of Robinson Publishing Ltd, 1992
Robinson Publishing
7 Kensington Church Court
London W8 4SP

Copyright © Robinson Publishing 1992

Illustrations courtesy of Mary Evans Picture Library

Cover picture Rasputin and Ku Klux Klan, Topham

ISBN 0 75251 632 9

A copy of the British Library Cataloguing in Publication Data is
available from the British Library

Printed and Bound in the EC

Contents

Cults and Fanatics

WORLD FAMOUS
CULTS AND FANATICS

Chapter One

Miracles Sometimes Happen

There is no way in which we can dismiss the idea that certain people can perform "miracles". And if that is true, then we cannot dismiss all "messiahs" as fakes. Perhaps they are people who sense that human beings possess extraordinary powers, and realize that the best way to develop them is to try to live the "religious life", and to persuade as many of their fellow creatures as possible to do the same thing. There are even cases where the powers of such people seem to live on after their death, as in the odd case of the Deacon of Paris.

Saint Joseph of Copertino and the Deacon of Paris demonstrate that miracles can happen. What seems stranger still is that the "miracle worker" need not be a genuine saint. Grigory Rasputin, the man who has been described as the "evil messiah" of pre-revolutionary Russia, was a bewildering mixture of saint and sinner.

The Day of Judgement According to William Miller

On 22 October, 1843, crowds of men and women gathered on a hilltop in Massachussetts, led by their prophet William Miller. In the previous year, Miller, a farmer and an ardent student of the *Book of Daniel*, had arrived at the conclusion that the end of the world was at hand, and that Christ was about to return to earth. One man

3

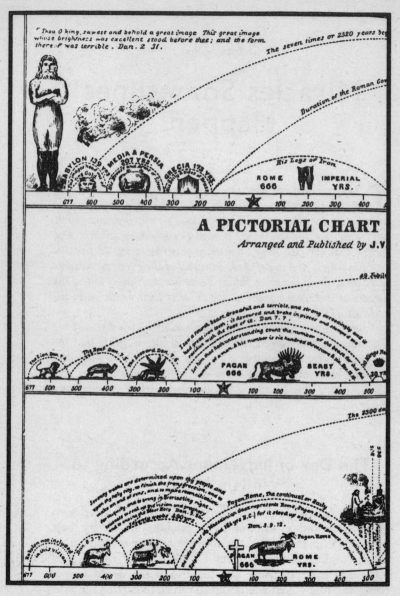

A Millerite chart of the visions and prophecies of Daniel.

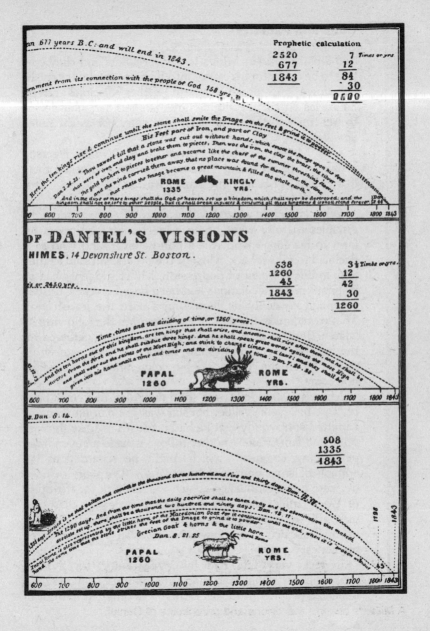

an 677 years B.C. and will end in 1843.

ernment from its connection with the people of God 158 yrs.

Prophetic calculation

```
2520        7  Times or yrs
 677       12
1843       84
           30
          ____
          2520
```

Here the ten kings rise & continue until the stone shall smite the Image on the feet & grind it to powder

His Feet part of Iron, and part of Clay

Dan 2 34. 35. "Thou sawest till that a stone was cut out without hands, which smote the Image upon his feet that were of iron and clay and brake them to pieces; Then was the iron, the clay the brass, the silver, the gold broken to pieces together and became like the chaff of the summer threshing floors; and the wind carried them away, that no place was found for them, and the stone that smote the Image became a great mountain & filled the whole earth

ROME **KINGLY**
1335 **YRS.**

And in the days of these kings shall the God of heaven, set up a kingdom, which shall never be destroyed: and the kingdom shall not be left to other people, but it shall break in pieces & consume all these kingdoms & it shall stand forever.

```
600  700  800  900  1000  1100  1200  1300  1400  1500  1600  1700  1800 1843
```

OF DANIEL'S VISIONS

HIMES, 14 Devonshire St. Boston.

or 2450 yrs.

```
 538        3½ Times or yrs
1260       12
  45       42
____       30
1843     ____
         1260
```

Time, times and the dividing of time, or 1260 years

out of this kingdom, are ten kings that shall arise, and another shall rise after them; and he shall be diverse from the first and he shall subdue three kings. And he shall speak great words against the Most High, and think to change times and laws; and they shall be given into his hand until a time and times and the dividing of time. Dan. 7. 24. 25.

PAPAL **ROME**
1260 **YRS.**

```
600  700  800  900  1000  1100  1200  1300  1400  1500  1600  1700  1800 1843
```

Dan. 8. 14.

```
 508
1335
____
1843
```

and pierced is he that sanctuary and cometh to the thousand three hundred and five and thirty days. Dan. 12. 12.

The 1290 days. And from the time that the daily sacrifice shall be taken away and the abomination that maketh desolate set up, there shall be a thousand two hundred and ninety days. Dan. 12. 11.

also represented by the little horn, of the Macedonian Goat for it continued until the end, when it is broken without the same time that the stone strikes the feet of the Image to grind it to powder.

Grecian Goat & horns & the little horn.
Dan. 8. 21. 25.

PAPAL **ROME**
1260 **YRS.**

```
600  700  800  900  1000  1100  1200  1300  1400  1500  1600  1700  1800 1843
```

tied a pair of turkey wings to his shoulders and climbed a tree to be ready for his ascent into heaven; unfortunately, he fell down and broke his arm. Other disciples carried umbrellas to aid the flight. One woman had tied herself to her trunk so that it would accompany her as she sailed upward.

One Millerite met the writer Ralph Waldo Emerson walking with his friend Theodore Parker, and asked them if they did not realize the world was about to end. "That doesn't affect me", said Parker, "I live in Boston."

When midnight passed with no sign of Armageddon, the disciples ruefully went home. One farmer had given his farm to his son — who was a non-believer, and who now declined to give it back. Most of the others had sold all they had. In this moment of depression, Miller suddenly had an inspiration: his calculations had been based on the Christian year, and no doubt he should have used the Jewish year. That would make the date of Armageddon the following 22 March. On that date, his followers once more gathered for the last Trumpet. Still nothing happened. One man wrote sadly: "Still in the cold world! No deliverance — the Lord did not come."

Miller's 50,000 followers soon dwindled to a small band of "true believers". Miller himself was not among them; he admitted sorrowfully that he had made his mistake through pride and fanaticism. Another follower made an even more penetrating comment, which might be regarded as the epitaph of any number of "messiahs": "We were deluded by mere human influence, which we mistook for the Spirit of God." Miller died five years later, a deeply chastened man, who recognized that he had been wasting his time in his Biblical calculations. Few other messiahs have possessed his honesty.

In fact, very few had his opportunity, for a large proportion of them have died ignominiously. In 1172, an unnamed prophet from the Yemen was dragged in front of

William Miller, leader of the "Millerites".

the Caliph, who demanded proof that he was a messenger from God. "That is easy", replied the prophet, "Cut off my head and I shall return to life." "That would indeed be a sign", said the Caliph, "and if you can do as you say, I will become your follower." Whereupon he signalled to his headsman. The head of the prophet rolled on the floor, and — predictably — the messiah failed to keep his promise.

The word messiah means "anointed" in Hebrew, and refers to the Jewish belief that King David will one day return and lead his people to victory. (Christ means the same thing in Greek.) The prophet Isaiah announced triumphantly that "unto us a child is born", and that the Messiah would take the "government upon his shoulders". Isaiah was writing roughly around 700 BC, after the Assyrians had conquered Israel and led its people (including the mythical "lost tribes") into exile. Ever since then, certain men have become possessed of the conviction that they are the promised Messiah, and ordered their disciples to follow them to victory and kingship. None has so far succeeded.

In the first millennium, it was widely believed that the year AD 1,000 would mark the end of the world. It failed to

At the Kofuku temple in Nara, Japan, a resentful
priest named Kurodo decided to play an
embarrassing trick on his fellow priests. At the
side of a pond near the temple, Kurodo set up a
placard that read: "On 3 March, a dragon shall
ascend from this pond." The effect was just
what he had expected. News of the placard
spread far and wide, and people talked of
nothing but dragons. On 3 March the pond was
surrounded by thousands of people from all the
neighbouring provinces. The day was sunny and
peaceful. By noon nothing had happened, and
the priests were beginning to feel worried. If no
dragon appeared, they would lose face.
Suddenly, a cloud drifted across the sky. A wind
sprang up. The day became darker, and a storm
broke. Rain fell in torrents and lightning flashed.
Before Kurodo's startled eyes, a smoky shape
like an enormous black dragon rose out of the
pond and up into the clouds. This story may or
may not be true. It was written by the great
Japanese author Akutagawa, who probably based
it on a tradition of the Kofuku temple.

materialize, but there was plenty of war and bloodshed –
the Crusades, for example – to encourage the believers to
feel that the end was nigh. The rollcall of those who – like
William Miller – have announced the end of the world is
impressive, as we shall see in this book.

Women have also been among these prophets of the new
Millennium, and a few have shown even greater fanaticism
than their male counterparts. Perhaps the most gruesome
example is the German prophetess Margaret Peter.

The Crucifixion of Margaret Peter

In the week after Easter, 1823, a horrible ceremony took place in a house in Wildisbuch, on the German-Swiss border. A twenty-nine year old woman named Margaret Peter, who was regarded as a holy woman by her disciples, announced that she had decided that she had to be crucified if Satan was to be defeated. Her sister Elizabeth immediately begged to be allowed to take her place. To demonstrate her sincerity, she picked up a mallet and struck herself on the head with it. Margaret then shouted: "It has been revealed to me that Elizabeth shall sacrifice herself", and she hit her sister on the head with a hammer. Then the remaining ten people in the room — including Margaret's other brothers and sisters — proceeded to beat Elizabeth with crowbars, hammers and wedges. "Don't worry", Margaret shouted, "I will raise her from the dead." One tremendous blow finally shattered Elizabeth's skull.

"Now *I* must die", Margaret told them. "You must crucify me." Following her sister's example, she picked up a hammer and hit herself on the head, then ordered the others to make a cross out of loose floorboards. When it was ready, she sent her sister Susanna downstairs to fetch nails. When Susanna returned, Margaret was lying on the floor on the cross. "Nail me to it", she ordered. "Don't be afraid. I will rise in three days." Two followers obediently nailed her elbows to the cross. The sight of the blood made them hesitate, and one was sick. Margaret encouraged them. "I feel no pain. Go on. Drive a nail through my heart." They drove nails through both her breasts, and a girl called Ursula tried to drive a knife through her heart. It bent against one of her ribs. Her brother Conrad, unable to stand the sight any longer, picked up a hammer and smashed in her skull.

The ten remaining disciples then went to eat their midday meal. They were exhausted but had no doubt that

Margaret and Elizabeth would be among them again in three days time. The deaths had taken place on Saturday; that meant Margaret and Elizabeth were due to arise on Tuesday.

But as the disciples sat around the battered corpses on Tuesday morning, no sign of life answered their prayers. Meanwhile, the local pastor, who had heard about the "sacrifice" from another disciple, called in the police. (He had known about the deaths for two days, but felt he had to give Margaret time to make good her promise.) The disciples were arrested, and taken to prison. They were tried in Zurich that December, and were all sentenced to varying prison terms.

The Death of Joanna Southcott

Sometimes, the prophet – or prophetess – loses faith at the last moment, but even when that happens, the disciples remain immune to doubt. When the English prophetess Joanna Southcott lay on her deathbed in 1814, she suddenly announced to her dismayed followers that her life's work now appeared a delusion. Although Joanna was a virgin, she had been convinced that she was about to give birth to the "child" foretold by Isaiah. And when one of her followers reminded her that she was carrying the Messiah (called Shiloh) in her womb, Joanna's tears suddenly changed to smiles.

After her death a few days later, her followers kept her body warm for three days as she had instructed them – then summoned a small army of medical men to remove the Christ child from her womb. The smell of putrefying flesh filled the room as the surgeon made the first incision, and some of the disciples hastily lit pipes to cover the smell. But when the womb was opened, there was obviously no baby there.

Does a place of worship have more intense thought fields than ordinary buildings? Can this explain the incredible case of the doll with human hair that keeps on growing?

The story comes from northern Japan and started in 1938. In that year Eikichi Suzuki took a ceramic doll to the temple in the village of Monji-Saiwai Cho for safekeeping. It had been a treasured possession of his beloved sister Kiku, who had died nineteen years before at the age of three. Suzuki kept it carefully in a box with the ashes of his dead sister.

Suzuki went off to World War II and didn't return for the doll until 1947. When he opened the box in the presence of the priest, they discovered that the doll's hair had grown down to its shoulders. A skin specialist from the Hokkaido University medical faculty said it was human hair.

The doll was placed on the altar, and its hair continued to grow. It is still growing, and is now almost waist length. The temple has become a place of pilgrimage for worshippers who believe the doll is a spiritual link with Buddha.

The priest of Monji-Saiwai Cho thinks that the little girl's soul somehow continues to live through the doll she loved so much.

"Damn me", said a doctor, "if the child is not *gone*." These words filled the disciples with new hope. Obviously, he meant that the child *had* been there, but had now been transferred to heaven. And even today, there are a small

Joanna Southcott.

number of followers of Joanna Southcott — they call themselves the Panacea Society — who believe that when her mysterious box is opened — a box supposed to contain her secret writings — all sin and wickedness in the world will suddenly disappear.

It is tempting to dismiss all these prophets and would-be saints as frauds or madmen. But that would undoubtedly be a mistake. Consider, for example, the strange case of Joseph of Copertino.

The Flying Monk

Giuseppe Desa was born in Apulia, Italy, in 1603, a strange, sickly boy who became known as "Open Mouth" because his mouth usually hung open; one commentator remarks that "he was not far from what today we should call a state of feeble-mindedness"; a bishop described him as *idiota* (although the word meant innocent rather than idiotic). He was subject to "ecstasies" and, even as a teenager, given to ascetic self-torments that undermined his health. At the age of seventeen he was accepted into the Capuchin order, but dismissed eight months later because of total inability to concentrate. Not long after, the order of Conventuals near Copertino accepted him as a stable boy, and at twenty-two he became a Franciscan priest. He continued to starve and flagellate himself, acquiring a reputation for holiness. Then one day, in the midst of his prayers after mass, he floated off the ground and landed on the altar in a state of ecstasy. He was unburned by candle flames, and flew back to his previous place.

Sent to see the Pope, he was again seized by such rapture that he rose in the air. His flying fits seem to have been always associated with the state that the Hindus called *samadhi*, ecstasy. His levitations ceased for two years when a hostile superior went out of his way to humiliate and persecute him; but after a holiday in Rome as the guest of the superior of the order, and an enthusiastic reception by the people of Assisi, he regained his good spirits and sailed fifteen yards to embrace the image of the Virgin on the altar.

He seems to have been a curious but simple case; floating in the air when in a state of delight seems to have been his sole accomplishment. The ecstasy did not have to be religious; on one occasion, when shepherds were playing their pipes in church on Christmas Eve, he began to dance for sheer joy, then flew on to the high altar, without knocking over any of the burning candles. Oddly enough, Saint Joseph could control his flights. On one occasion, when he had flown past lamps and ornaments that blocked the way to the altar, his superior called him back, and he flew back to the place he had vacated. When a

The flying Capuchin monk Guiseppe Desa.

Flying saucer cults exist all around the world. Most hold the view put forward in Erich Von Dänlken's book *The Chariots of the Gods?*: that the human concept of "God" was created when we were visited by alien beings at some stage in our pre-history.

UFOs reached the public consciousness during the late 1940s. A spate of sightings seemed to loose a tidal wave of stories involving abduction by aliens and mysterious landings. Throughout the Fifties, pulp science fiction publications pushed the idea of mysterious alien races that hang around in earth's upper atmosphere planning our downfall. Strange mutilations of cattle in Texas were ascribed to them. More recently a series of "corn circles", bizarre asymmetric patterns composed of crushed crops, were said to be produced by their landings.

Believers in the UFO conspiracy maintain that witnesses to alien activities are visited by the mysterious Men In Black. These black-suited officials advise the witness to keep quiet about the sighting. Whether these are aliens in disguise or agents of government covert operations is not known – perhaps they are both.

The spiritual side of saucer cults tends to focus on the higher knowledge of alien beings conquering famine and war. Some believe that life on earth was "seeded" here millions of years ago by aliens, and that they will soon return to see how their experiment has gone. This idea actually forms the basis of the obscure-but-popular film "*2001 – A Space Odyssey*".

fellow monk remarked on the beauty of the sky, he shrieked and flew to the top of a nearby tree. He was also able to lift heavy weights; one story tells of how he raised a wooden cross that ten workmen were struggling to place in position, and flew with it to the hole that had been prepared for it. He was also able to make others float; he cured a demented nobleman by seizing his hair and flying into the air with him, remaining there a quarter of an hour, according to his biographer; on another occasion, he seized a local priest by the hand, and after dancing around with him, they both flew, hand in hand. When on his deathbed, at the age of sixty, the doctor in attendance observed, as he cauterized a septic leg, that Fr Joseph was floating in the air six inches above the chair. He died saying that he could hear the sounds and smell the scents of paradise.

What are we to make of such phenomena? It would be convenient if we could dismiss the whole thing as a pack of lies or as mass hysteria or hypnosis. We can certainly dismiss ninety-five per cent of the miracles attributed to the saints in this way without a twinge of conscience. (A typical example: St Dunstan of Glastonbury is reported to have changed the position of the church by pushing it.) But the evidence cannot be dismissed; it is overwhelming. His feats were witnessed by kings, dukes and philosophers (or at least one philosopher — Leibnitz). When his canonization was suggested, the Church started an investigation into his flights, and hundreds of depositions were taken. He became a saint a hundred and four years after his death.

The Miracles of Saint-Médard

The strange events that took place in the little Paris churchyard of Saint-Médard between 1727 and 1732 sound so incredible, so preposterous, that the modern reader is tempted to dismiss them as pure invention. This would be a mistake, for an impressive mass of documents, including accounts by doctors, magistrates and other respectable public figures, attests to their genuineness. The miracles undoubtedly took place. But no doctor, philosopher or scientist has even begun to explain them.

They began with the burial of François de Pâris, the Deacon of Paris, in May 1727. François was only thirty-seven years old, yet he was revered as a holy man, with powers of healing. He was a follower of Bishop Cornelius Jansen, who taught that men can be saved only by divine grace, not by their own efforts. The Deacon had no doubt whatever that his own healing powers came from God.

Great crowds followed his coffin, many weeping. It was laid in a tomb behind the high altar of Saint-Médard. Then the congregation filed past, laying their flowers on the corpse. A father supported his son, a cripple, as he leaned over the coffin. Suddenly, the child went into convulsions; he seemed to be having a fit. Several people helped to drag him, writhing, to a quiet corner of the church. Suddenly the convulsions stopped. The boy opened his eyes, looking around in bewilderment, and then slowly stood up. A look of incredulous joy crossed his face; then to the astonishment of the spectators he began to dance up and down, singing and laughing. His father found it impossible to believe, for the boy was using his withered right leg, which had virtually no muscles. Later it was claimed that the leg had become as strong and normal as the other.

The news spread. Within hours cripples, lepers, hunch-backs and blind men were rushing to the church. At first, few "respectable" people believed the stories of miraculous cures — the majority of the Deacon's followers were poor people. The rich preferred to leave their spiritual affairs in the hands of the Jesuits, who were more cultivated and worldly. But it soon became clear that ignorance and credulity could not be used as a blanket explanation for all the stories of marvels. Deformed limbs, it was said, were being straightened; hideous growths and cancers were disappearing without trace; horrible sores and wounds were healing instantly.

The Jesuits declared that the miracles were either a fraud or the work of the Devil; the result was that most of the better-off people in Paris flatly refused to believe that anything unusual was taking place in the churchyard of Saint-Médard. But a few men of intellect were drawn by curiosity, and they invariably returned from the churchyard profoundly shaken. Sometimes they recorded their testimony in print: some, such as one Philippe Hecquet, attempted to explain the events by natural causes. Others, such as the Benedictine Bernard Louis de la Taste, attacked the people who performed the miracles on theological grounds, but were unable to expose any deception or error by them, or any error on the part of the witnesses. The accumulation of written testimony was such that David Hume, one of the greatest of philosophers, wrote in *An enquiry concerning human understanding* (1758):

> There surely never was a greater number of miracles ascribed to one person . . . But what is more extra-ordinary; many of the miracles were immediately proved upon the spot, before judges of unquestioned integrity, attested by witnesses of credit and distinction, in a learned age . . . Where shall we find such a number of circumstances, agreeing to the corrobora-tion of one fact?

One of those who investigated happenings was a lawyer named Louis Adrien de Paige. When he told his friend, the magistrate Louis-Basile Carré de Montgéron, what he had seen, the magistrate assured him patronizingly that he had been taken in by conjuring tricks — the kind of "miracles" performed by tricksters at fairgrounds. But he finally agreed to go with Paige to the churchyard, if only for the pleasure of pointing out how the lawyer had been deceived. They went there on the morning of 7 September 1731. And de Montgéron left the churchyard a changed man — he even endured prison rather than deny what he had seen that day.

The first thing the magistrate saw when he entered the churchyard was a number of women writhing on the ground, twisting themselves into the most startling shapes, sometimes bending backward until the backs of their heads touched their heels. These ladies were all wearing a long cloth undergarment that fastened around the ankles. Paige explained that this was now obligatory for all women who wished to avail themselves of the Deacon's miraculous powers. In the early days, when women had stood on their heads or bent their bodies convulsively, prurient young men had begun to frequent the churchyard to view the spectacle.

However, there was no lack of male devotees of the deceased Abbé to assist in the activities of the churchyard. Montgéron was shocked to see that some of the women and girls were being sadistically beaten — at least, that is what at first appeared to be going on. Men were striking them with heavy pieces of wood and iron. Other women lay on the ground, apparently crushed under immensely heavy weights. One girl was naked to the waist: a man was gripping her nipples with a pair of iron tongs and twisting them violently. Paige explained that none of these women felt any pain; on the contrary, many begged for more blows. And an incredible number of them were cured of deformities or diseases by this violent treatment.

In another part of the churchyard, they saw an attractive pink-cheeked girl of about nineteen, who was sitting at a trestle table and eating. That seemed normal enough until Montgéron looked more closely at the food on the plate, and realized from its appearance as well as from the smell that reached him that it was human excrement. In between mouthfuls of this sickening fare she drank a yellow liquid, which Paige explained was urine. The girl had come to the churchyard to be cured of what we would now call a neurosis: she had to wash her hands hundreds of times a day, and was so fastidious about her food that she would taste nothing that had been touched by another human hand. The Deacon had indeed cured her. Within days she was eating excrement and drinking urine, and did so with every sign of enjoyment. Such cases might not be remarkable in asylums; but what was more extraordinary — indeed, preposterous — was that after one of these meals she opened her mouth as if to be sick, and milk came pouring out. Monsieur Paige had collected a cupful; it was apparently perfectly ordinary cow's milk.

After staggering away from the eater of excrement, Montgéron had to endure a worse ordeal. In another part of the churchyard, a number of women had volunteered to cleanse suppurating wounds and boils by sucking them clean. Trying hard to prevent himself vomiting, Montgéron watched as someone unwound a dirty bandage from the leg of a small girl; the smell was horrible. The leg was a festering mass of sores, some so deep that the bone was visible. The woman who had volunteered to clean it was one of the *convulsionnaires* — she had been miraculously cured and converted by her bodily contortions, and God had now chosen her to demonstrate how easily human beings' disgust can be overcome. Yet even she blenched as she saw and smelt the gangrened leg. She cast her eyes up to heaven, prayed silently for a moment, then bent her head and began to lap, swallowing the septic matter. When she moved her face farther down the child's leg Montgéron could see that the wound was now clean. Paige assured him that the girl would almost certainly be cured when the treatment was complete.

What Montgéron saw next finally shattered his resistance and convinced him that he was witnessing something of profound significance. A sixteen-year-old girl named Gabrielle Moler had arrived, and the interest she excited made Montgéron aware that, even among this crowd of miraculous freaks, she was a celebrity. She removed her cloak and lay on the ground, her skirt modestly round her ankles. Four men, each holding a pointed iron bar, stood over her. When the girl smiled at them they lunged down at her, driving their rods into her stomach. Montgéron had to be restrained from interfering as the rods went through the girl's dress and into her stomach. He looked for signs of blood staining her dress. But none came, and the girl looked calm and serene. Next the bars were jammed under her chin, forcing her head back. It seemed inevitable that they would penetrate through to her mouth; yet when the points were removed the flesh was unbroken. The men took up sharp-edged shovels, placed them against a breast, and then pushed with all their might; the girl went on smiling gently. The breast, trapped between shovels, should have been cut off, but it seemed impervious to the assault. Then the cutting edge of a shovel was placed against her throat, and the man wielding it did his best to cut off her head; he did not seem to be able even to dent her neck.

Dazed, Montgéron watched as the girl was beaten with a great iron truncheon shaped like a pestle. A stone weighing half a hundredweight (25 kilograms) was raised above her body and dropped repeatedly from a height of several feet. Finally, Montgéron watched her kneel in front of a blazing fire, and plunge her head into it. He could feel the heat from where he stood; yet her hair and eyebrows were not even singed. When she picked up a blazing chunk of coal and proceeded to eat it Montgéron could stand no more and left.

But he went back repeatedly, until he had enough materials for the first volume of an amazing book. He presented it to the king, Louis XV, who was so shocked and indignant that he had Montgéron thrown into prison. Yet Montgéron felt he had to "bear witness", and was to publish two more volumes following his release, full of precise scientific testimony concerning the miracles.

In the year following Montgéron's imprisonment, 1732, the Paris authorities decided that the scandal was becoming unbearable and closed down the churchyard. But the *convulsionnaires* had discovered that they could perform their miracles anywhere, and they continued for many years. A hardened sceptic, the scientist La Condamine, was as startled as Montgéron when, in 1759, he watched a girl named Sister Françoise being crucified on a wooden cross, nailed by the hands and feet over a period of several hours, and stabbed in the side with a spear. He noticed that all this obviously hurt the girl, and her wounds bled when the nails were removed; but she seemed none the worse for an ordeal that would have killed most people.

So what can we say of the miracles from the standpoint of the twentieth century? Some writers believe it was a kind of self-hypnosis. But while this could explain the excrement-eater and the woman who sucked festering wounds, it is less plausible in explaining Gabrielle Moler's feats of endurance. These remind us rather of descriptions of ceremonies of dervishes and fakirs: for example, J.G. Bennett in his autobiography *Witness* describes watching a dervish ritual in which a razor-sharp sword was placed across the belly of a naked man, and two heavy men jumped up and down on it — all without even marking the flesh. What seems to be at work here is some power of "mind over matter", deeper than mere hypnosis, which is not yet understood but obviously merits serious attention.

It would be absurd to stop looking for scientific explanations of the miracles of Saint-Médard. But let us not in the meantime deceive ourselves by accepting superficial "sceptical" explanations.

A Miraculous Cure

Josephine Hoare, a healthy girl of twenty-one, had been married for only six months when she developed chronic nephritis, a serious inflammation of the kidneys. Her family was told that she had no more than two years to live. At her mother's suggestion, she was taken to Lourdes.

At the famous French shrine, Josephine braved the icy waters of the spring. Although she felt peaceful, she was not conscious of any change. When she went home, however, her doctor said in amazement that the disorder seemed to have cleared. Her swollen legs returned to normal size, her blood pressure became normal, and her energy increased. But she was warned that pregnancy would certainly cause a relapse.

Several years passed. Then Josephine and her husband had the opportunity to revisit Lourdes, and Josephine lit a candle of thanksgiving. Soon after they got home, she felt a sharp pain in her back. Fearful that nephritis was recurring, she went to her doctor. His diagnosis was simply that she was six months pregnant — and she had had no relapse.

Josephine Hoare had her baby, a son, and remained in good health. For her and her family, the spring of Lourdes had produced a double miracle.

Search for a Missing Boy

In 1933 a six-year-old boy vanished from his home in Miège in the Swiss Alps. After an unsuccessful search for the boy, the town's mayor wrote to Abbé Mermet, who had often assisted police in locating missing people. The Abbé needed an article used by the missing person, a description of the last place he or she was seen, and a map of the surrounding area to do his work. He used a

Some groups believe that the Great Pyramid in Egypt had encoded within its measurements many great truths. Christian sects have maintained that it was not the Egyptians who built it at all but the Israelites. According to this theory the internal passageways of the Pyramid, measured in the correct units, are a three dimensional model of the history of the world up to Christ's birth. On a more secular level, twice the length of the base of the Pyramid divided by its height, again in the correct units, is supposed to approximate to *pi*. It is difficult to verify these statements as the nature of the correct units is a matter of conjecture, and the actual size of the Pyramid in any units is still problematic.

The Anglo-Israelite fundamentalist sect took the argument a stage further. Not only was the Pyramid not built by the Egptians; it was also not entirely correct to say the Israelites built it. According to the Anglo-Israelites, the Anglo-Saxon races of Britain and America were the only true tribe of Israel remaining. It was they who had built the Pyramid, as a warning that the world would end and that Christ would return on 20 August, 1953. When the date passed without significant upheaval, the Anglo-Israelites began to formulate the theory that the message of the Pyramid was not literal, but a religious metaphor . . .

pendulum and a form of dowsing to find the missing person.

After the Abbé applied his pendulum to the problem of the missing boy, he reported that the child had been carried away into the mountains by a large bird of prey, probably an eagle. He also said that the bird — although enormous — had dropped its load twice to rest and regain its strength.

There was no trace of the boy at the first place the Abbé indicated. A recent heavy snowfall prevented a thorough search at the second place, but the conclusion was that Abbé Mermet had made a mistake.

When the snow melted two weeks later, however, a gang of woodcutters found the torn and mangled body of a small boy. It was the missing child. The bird had apparently been prevented from completely savaging the child's body by the sudden heavy storm that had also hidden the forlorn evidence.

Scientific investigation established that the boy's shoes and clothes had not come into contact with the ground where the body was found. He could only have reached the remote spot by air — the pitiful victim of the bird of prey. Later the boy's father apologized to the Abbé for having doubted him.

Rasputin, "the Holy Sinner"

Grigory Rasputin's body was taken from the frozen river Neva, in Petrograd, on 1 January, 1917. He had been murdered three days before, and was one of the most notorious figures in Russia. Now that he was dead, he would become a legend all over the world — a symbol of evil, cunning, and lust. If ever you see a magazine story entitled "Rasputin, the Mad Monk", you can be sure it will be full of lurid details of how Rasputin spent his days in drunken carousing, his nights in sexual debauchery; how he deceived the Tsar and Tsarina into thinking he was a miracle worker; how he was the evil genius who brought about the Russian Revolution and the downfall of the

Rasputin surrounded by the adoring ladies of the Russian court.

Romanov dynasty. It is all untrue. Yet it makes such a good story that there is little chance that Rasputin will ever receive justice. The truth about him is that he really was a miracle worker and a man of strange powers. He was certainly no saint — very few magicians are — and tales of his heavy drinking and sexual prowess are undoubtedly based on fact. But he was no diabolical schemer.

Rasputin was born in the village of Pokrovskoe in 1870. His father was a fairly well-to-do peasant. As a young man, Rasputin had a reputation for wildness until he visited a monastery and spent four months there in prayer and meditation. For the remainder of his life, he was obsessed by religion. He married at nineteen and became a prosperous carter. Then the call came again; he left his family and took to the road as a kind of wandering monk. When eventually he returned, he was a changed man, exuding an extraordinarily powerful

It was November 1971 in London on a day like any other. In one of the city's underground stations, a train was approaching the platform. Suddenly a young man hurled himself directly into the path of the moving train. The horrified driver slammed on the brakes, certain that there was no way to stop the train before the man was crushed under the wheels. But miraculously the train did stop. The first carriage had to be jacked up to remove the badly injured man, but the wheels had not passed over him and he survived.

The young man turned out to be a gifted architect who was recovering from a nervous breakdown. His amazing rescue from death was based on coincidence. For the investigation of the accident revealed that the train had not stopped because of the driver's hasty braking. Seconds before, acting on an impulse and completely unaware of the man about to throw himself on the tracks, a passenger had pulled down the emergency handle, which automatically applies the brakes of the train. The passenger had no particular reason for doing so. In fact, the Transport Authority considered prosecuting him on the grounds that he had had no reasonable cause for using the emergency system!

magnetism. The young people of his village were fascinated by him. He converted one room in his house into a church, and it was always full. The local priest became envious of his following, however, and Rasputin was forced to leave home again.

Rasputin had always possessed the gift of second sight. One day during his childhood, this gift had revealed to him the identity of a peasant who had stolen a horse and hidden it in a barn. Now, on his second round of travels, he also began to develop extraordinary healing powers. He would kneel by the beds of the sick and pray; then he would lay hands on them, and cure many of them. When he came to St Petersburgh, probably late in 1903, he already had a reputation as a wonder worker. Soon he was accepted in aristocratic society in spite of his rough peasant manners.

It was in 1907 that he suddenly became the power behind the throne. Three years before, Tsarina Alexandra had given birth to a longed-for heir to the throne, Prince Alexei. But it was soon apparent that Alexei had inherited haemophilia, a disease that prevents the blood from clotting, and from which a victim may bleed to death even with a small cut. At the age of three the prince fell and bruised himself so severely that an internal haemorrhage developed. He lay in a fever for days, and doctors despaired of his life. Then the Tsarina recalled the man of God she had met two years earlier, and sent for Rasputin. As soon as he came in he said calmly: "Do not worry the child. He will be all right." He laid his hand on the boy's forehead, sat down on the edge of the bed, and began to talk to him in a quiet voice. Then he knelt and prayed. In a few minutes the boy was in a deep and peaceful sleep, and the crisis was over.

Henceforward the Tsarina felt a powerful emotional dependence on Rasputin – a dependence nourished by the thinly veiled hostility with which Alexandra, a German, was treated at court. Rasputin's homely strength brought her a feeling of security. The Tsar also began to confide in Rasputin, who became a man of influence at court. Nicholas II was a poor ruler, not so much cruel as weak, and too indecisive to stem the rising tide of social discontent. His opponents began to believe that Rasputin was responsible for some of the Tsar's reactionary policies, and a host of powerful enemies began to gather. On several occasions the Tsar had to give way to the pressure and order Rasputin to leave the city. On one such occasion, the young prince fell and hurt himself again. For several days he tossed in agony, until he seemed too weak to survive. The Tsarina dispatched a telegram to Rasputin, and he telegraphed back: "The illness is not as dangerous as it seems." From the moment it was received, the prince began to recover.

World War I brought political revolution and military catastrophe to Russia. Its outbreak was marked by a strange coincidence: Rasputin was stabbed by a madwoman at precisely the same moment as the Archduke Franz Ferdinand was shot at Sarajevo. Rasputin hated war, and might have been able to dissuade the Tsar from leading Russia into the conflict. But he was in bed recovering from his stab wound when the moment of decision came.

Rasputin's end was planned by conspirators in the last days of 1916. He was lured to a cellar by Prince Felix Yussupov, a man he trusted. After feeding him poisoned cakes, Yussupov shot him in the back; then Rasputin was beaten with an iron bar. Such was his immense vitality that he was still alive when the murderers dropped him through the hole in the ice into the Neva. Among his papers was found a strange testament addressed to the Tsar. It stated that he had a strong feeling he would die by violence before January 1, 1917, and that if he were killed by peasants, the Tsar would reign for many years to come; but, if he were killed by aristocrats – as he was – then "none of your children or relations will remain alive for more than two years". He was right. The Tsar and his family were all murdered in July 1918 – an amazing example, among many, of Rasputin's gift of precognition.

The lesson is simple: many messiahs are deluded, but it would be a mistake to dismiss them all as madmen.

Chapter Two

Waiting for the Warrior-King

A lthough many of the great mystics spent their lives as members of the Church, they did not believe that the Church was essential for "salvation". Man can know God directly, without the need for priests and sacraments. Some of them — like the thirteenth century mystic Meister Eckhart — came dangerously close to being excommunicated, or even burned at the stake. (Eckhart was tried for heresy but died before he was condemned — which he was.)

It was only one step from this belief that man has direct access to God, to the belief that there is no such thing as sin. If man is truly free, then he has choice, and if he chooses to reject the idea that something is sinful — for example, sexual promiscuity or incest — no authority has a right to tell him he is a sinner. Preachers of this doctrine were known as Brethren of the Free Spirit.

Was Jesus a Messiah?

T he answer to that question may seem obvious, for his followers certainly regarded him as *the* Messiah. But did Jesus agree with them? The answer is: probably not. When his disciple Peter told him: "They call you the Christ, the Messiah", Jesus advised him to be silent. The claim obviously embarrassed him.

Why? Because, as we have seen, the Jewish craving for a Messiah arose out of the longing for someone to lead them

to victory. After the Assyrian invasion, the Jews became a
conquered people, oppressed by a series of more powerful
nations: the Seleucids (descendants of Alexander the Great),
the Babylonians, the Egyptians, the Romans. For the same
reason, the British of a thousand years later came to believe
firmly that King Arthur would return to throw off the
foreign yoke. Jesus had no desire to be regarded as a
military commander, which is what the word Messiah
originally implied.

What is difficult for modern Christians to grasp is that
Jesus was only one of many Hebrew prophets who were
believed to be the Messiah; the historian Josephus mentions
several of them. He regarded them all as charlatans and
agitators. Christians later changed Josephus's text, in which
Jesus is described as a small man with a hunched back and a
half-bald head, to read: "six feet tall, well grown, with a
venerable face, handsome nose . . . curly hair the colour of
unripe hazel nuts . . .", and various other details that
transform the unprepossessing little man into the early
Christian equivalent of a film star. So all the writings
about Jesus have to be treated with great caution; the
later Christians were quite unscrupulous in changing anything that disagreed with their own image of "the Messiah".

But if Jesus declined to be regarded as a military leader,
why did anyone pay any attention to him? The answer is
that he announced that the end of the world was about to
take place, and that this would happen *within the lifetime of
people then alive*. This is why he told them to take no
thought for the morrow, and that God would provide. The
world would soon be ending.

It is also important to understand that it was the Jews
themselves, not their Roman conquerors, who disliked
Jesus. The Sadducees, who loved Greek culture and dis-
believed in life after death, thought him an uncultivated
fanatic. The Pharisees, who regarded themselves as the
guardians of the Law, reacted angrily to Jesus's attacks on

them as narrow-minded and old-fashioned. The Zealots wanted to see the Romans conquered and thrown out of Palestine, and had no patience with a Messiah who preached peace and love. While Jesus was wandering around the countryside preaching in the open air, no one worried about him. But when he rode into Jerusalem on a donkey (fulfilling the prophesy of Isaiah) and was greeted with enthusiasm by the people, the Jewish establishment became alarmed. And when Jesus threw the money changers out of the temple, they saw the writing on the wall, and had him arrested. The arrest had to take place in a garden at night to avoid causing trouble.

Of the four Gospels, only one, that of John, claims to be that of an eyewitness. When Jesus is taken before Caiaphas, the high priest asks him about his teachings, and Jesus tells him to ask those who have heard him — to the indignation of the high priest's servant, who slaps his face and tells him not to be impertinent. It is in the other three Gospels — by writers who do not claim to have known him — that Jesus answers the question about whether he is the son of God by replying that he is "Son of Man" who will sit on the right hand of God.

In John's account, Pilate asks him if he is the king of the Jews, and Jesus replies that his kingdom is not of this world — meaning, in effect, that Pilate should not imagine he is claiming any political leadership. "I have come into the world to bear witness to the truth." There is certainly nothing here about claiming to be the Messiah.

To Pilate's disgust, the Jews then demanded Jesus's execution, declining to allow him to be pardoned in honour of Passover. And so Jesus died, like so many other messiahs and political agitators, by crucifixion.

How, then, did Christianity go on to conquer the world? The answer lies partly in the many stories of miracles that circulated about Jesus — including the story that he had risen from the dead. A Jewish sect called the Messianists (or

Nasoraeans) believed that Jesus would return and lead them against the Romans. At this point, a convert to Christianity named Paul produced a strange and mystical new version of Jesus's teaching that seemed to have very little to do with anything Jesus had actually said. Paul declared that Jesus was the Son of God (which Jesus had denied) who had been sent to redeem Man from the sin of Adam, and that anyone who believed in Jesus was "saved". In fact, Jesus had preached salvation through the efforts of the individual, and insisted that the Kingdom of God is within everybody. But since there was still a widespread belief that the End of the World would occur within a year or so, Paul's version of the Christian message was a powerful incentive to belief. The Messianists regarded such a notion as absurd and blasphemous, and since they were politically stronger than Paul's Christians, it looked as if their version would triumph.

However, as it happened, the Messianists were among those wiped out by Titus, the son of the Roman emperor Vespasian, who was sent to put down the latest rebellion. He did more than that; he destroyed the Temple and carried its treasures back to Rome. Paul's "Christians" were so widely scattered that they were relatively immune from massacre. And so, by a historical accident, Paul's version of Christianity became the official version, and the "vicarious atonement" – the notion that Jesus died on the cross to redeem man from the sin of Adam – became the basis of the religion that went on to conquer the world.

By the year AD 100 it was obvious that the world was not going to end within the lifetime of Jesus's contemporaries, and that Jesus, like so many other messiahs, had quite simply been wrong. But by that time, Christianity was too powerful to die out. It was now a political force, the focus of all the dissatisfaction of the underdogs and victims of Roman brutality. The belief now spread that the end of the world would occur in the year AD 1000. And, as we have seen, there was so much violence, pestilence and bloodshed around that time that the believers had no doubt that the end was just around the corner.

Simon Bar Kochba

But even before the millennium, there were plenty of messiahs. In AD 132, a Jewish revolutionary named Simon Bar Kochba led a revolt against the Romans in Judaea when he learned that the Emperor Hadrian intended to build a temple dedicated to Jupiter on the site of the temple that had been destroyed by Titus. A celebrated student of the Talmud, (the Jewish book of law) Rabbi Akiva, told Simon Bar Kochba: "You are the Messiah." And Bar Kochba behaved exactly as a Jewish Messiah was expected to behave (and as Jesus had failed to behave); he seized town and villages from the Romans, had his own head stamped on the coinage, and built fortresses. But he stood no real chance against the Romans, with their highly trained troops. It took Julius Severus three and a half years to destroy the rebels, and in that time he destroyed fifty fortresses and 985 villages, and killed over half a million people. Since Bar Kochba's men were guerillas, and guerillas survive by being supported by sympathizers, Severus set out to kill all the sympathizers. He finally killed Bar Kochba himself in the fortress of Bethar, and renamed Jerusalem Aelia Capitolana. So one more Messiah was proved to be mortal after all. The Jews were so shattered by this defeat that there were no more Jewish messiahs for many centuries.

Moses of Crete

In about AD 435, an unnamed messiah from Crete, who called himself Moses, announced that, like his predecessor, he would lead his followers back to the Promised Land, causing the sea to part for them so they could walk on the bottom. Hundreds of followers gathered on the seashore, and Moses raised his arms and ordered the sea to separate. Then he shouted the order to march into the waves. They obeyed him, but the sea ignored his order, and many of his followers were drowned. Moses may have been drowned with them; at all events, he disappeared.

The Christ of Gevaudon

In AD 591, an unnamed messiah began to wander around France. This man had apparently had a nervous breakdown after being surrounded by a swarm of flies in a forest; he recovered after two years and became a preacher, clad himself in animal skins, and wandered down through Arles to the district of Gevaudon in the Cevennes (noted later for a famous case of a werewolf). He declared he was Christ, had a companion called Mary, and healed the sick by touching them. (As we have seen in the case of Rasputin, this may be a natural gift.) His followers were mostly the very poor, and they often waylaid travellers (most of whom would be rich) and seized their money. The Messiah redistributed it to the poor. His army of 3,000 became so powerful that most towns lost no time in acknowledging him as the Christ.

Before he arrived at the cathedral city of La Puy he quartered his army in neighbouring halls and churches, and sent messengers to announce his coming to Bishop Aurelius. When these messengers appeared in front of the

The inhabitants of the Melanesian islands in the Pacific have, since their first contact with western travellers, developed the so-called "cargo cults". Cargo refers in the islanders' pidgin to goods of any kind given by visitors.

First contact occurred with the arrival of the Russian Count Nikolai Miklouho-Maclay in 1871. He was received as a god, due to the incredible nature of his transport, a Russian frigate, and his gifts, which were amazing to a culture that was still in the Stone Age. German traders and Christian missionaries only served to reinforce the natives awe and faith. The basic tenets of the religion became set: visitors who give "cargo" are good, those who do not are evil, as they withhold what are seen as spiritual gifts.

In 1940 the Americans built a military base on the Melanesian island of Tanna in the southern New Hebrides. Cargo planes zoomed in and out leaving radios, canned beer and other western necessities. The natives observed the American service men in uniform, and wishing to bring more planes and enjoy similar luxuries they improvised uniforms and spoke into empty beer cans, as they had seen the Americans speak into microphones.

What began as adoration and emulation soon turned to dissatisfaction as their rituals failed to get the desired response. The faith changed its nature, becoming a conviction that the present western presence on the island was of the wrong kind. Soon a messiah would come to give the natives what the Americans refused to give

them. John Frum or Jonfrum was the name that
the natives gave this messiah, although the
reason is not clear. Some say that Frum is a
corruption of broom, to sweep away the white
man. Others put forward the simpler
explanation that the name is derived from "John
from America". He is described as a small man
with bleached hair, a high-pitched voice and a
coat with shiny buttons.

The cult persists in many different forms on
each of the remote Melanesian islands. What
began as simple worship of westerners has
developed into an entire liberation theology in a
very short time: John Frum will one day arrive
and hand over all of the "cargo" to the natives,
while getting rid of the westerners. After that
the islanders would live on as normal, only
richer and happier than before.

bishop stark naked and turned somersaults, he decided it
was time to end the career of this dangerous and disre-
spectful rebel. He sent his men to meet him, apparently to
welcome him, and as one of them bowed down as if to kiss
the Messiah's knees, they grabbed him and dragged him to
the ground, his companions rushed forward and hacked the
Messiah to pieces. With their "Christ" dead, the rebellious
followers soon dispersed. Mary was apparently tortured
until she revealed the "diabolic devices" that had given the
Messiah his power — St Gregory of Tours, who recounts the
story, naturally assumed that it was all the Devil's work. But
he also records that the Messiah's followers continued to
believe in him to the day they died, and to maintain that he
was the Christ.

A century and a half later, about 742, a messiah called Aldebert, who came from Soissons, announced that he was a saint; his followers built chapels for him which he named after himself. He claimed to own a letter from Jesus himself. Pope Zachary was so worried about "Saint" Aldebert's influence that he tried hard to capture him, and, when that failed, excommunicated him. Adelbert went on for at least two more years, and seems to have died of natural causes.

Eudo de Stella

Three centuries later, another messiah called Eon or Eudo de Stella was less lucky. He gathered hordes of disciples in Britanny, and organized his followers into a Church with archbishops and bishops. Unlike Jesus of Nazareth, he had no hesitation in declaring that he was the son of God. AD 1144 was a good year for a messiah to acquire followers, for an appalling winter caused multitudes to starve. Eon's followers lived in the forest, and ravaged the countryside, living mainly by plunder. But in 1148, he was finally taken prisoner by soldiers of the Archbishop of Rouen, and imprisoned in a tower, where he was starved to death. His followers refused to renounce him, and the "bishops" and "archbishops" were burned alive in the now traditional Christian spirit.

Tanchelm

One of the most remarkable messiahs of the twelfth century, Tanchelm of Antwerp, was already dead by then. He seems to have started his career as a monk, then become a diplomat working for Count Robert of Flanders, trying to persuade the Pope to hand over some of Utrecht to Count Robert. The Pope refused, and when Count Robert died, Tanchelm's career as a diplomat came to an end. He became a wandering preacher, making his headquarters in Antwerp.

Tanchelm seems to have possessed what all messiahs possess: tremendous powers as a preacher and orator. We also have to remember that a large part of his audience would be ignorant peasants who had never heard a really good preacher. As Tanchelm addressed them in the open fields, dressed as a monk, the audiences reacted like modern teenagers to a pop idol. He denounced the Church for its corruption, and told them that if the sacraments were administered by sinful priests, they would fail to work. So many were convinced that the churches were soon empty. And when Tanchelm told his followers not to pay taxes to the church (called tithes), they were delighted to follow his advice.

Was Tanchelm a charlatan, or did he really believe he was a messiah? He certainly felt that he had a right to live like a king. He dressed magnificently, and was always surrounded by a large retinue, including twelve men who were supposed to be the twelve disciples. One day he announced that he would become betrothed to the Virgin Mary, and held a ceremony in which he and a sacred statue were joined together in front of a vast crowd, who offered their jewellery as an engagement present.

With so many followers, the Church could do nothing about him; he held Utrecht, Antwerp and large areas of the countryside. Finally, about AD 1115, he was killed – like the Messiah of Gevaudon – by treachery, being stabbed by a priest who had been allowed to approach him. But his influence remained as powerful as ever, and it took another "miracle worker", Norbert of Xanten (who was regarded with favour by the Church) to finally "de-convert" his followers in Antwerp and restore power to the Church.

Rebellion, Mysticism and Sex.

How did these "messiahs" become so powerful? To begin
with, all of them had the gift of preaching. But it was more
than that. The Christian Church, which began as a poor and
persecuted organization whose leaders were thrown to the
lions, suddenly became the official religion of Rome in AD
313, under the Emperor Constantine. As soon as they
gained power, the Christians began to behave far worse
than their enemies, destroying pagan temples, burning
heretics, and squabbling amongst themselves. In effect,
the Church became the supreme dictator. And the poor,
ordered to go to church every Sunday, groaning under
heavy taxes and forced to pay to have their sins forgiven,
became increasingly disenchanted with their spiritual masters. But there was nothing they could do; the Church
exerted the same iron grip as the Nazis in Germany or the
Communists in Stalin's Russia.

This is why rebel messiahs found an eager audience.
Like Jesus, they attacked the establishment and declared
that the "law" was less important than the spirit. Besides,
there had always been a strong tradition of Mysticism in
the Church. Mystics were men who had experienced
moments of overwhelming joy and illumination in which
they felt they had seen God. The mystics taught that
every man has a divine spark, and that therefore, in a
sense, every man is God — or contains a fragment of God.
They also believed that all Nature is an expression of God
— in fact some (called Pantheists) believed that Nature *is*
God. One of the greatest of the early mystics, Dionysius
the Areopagite (around AD 500) taught that God is a kind
of emptiness or darkness, and can only be reached by
recognizing that God is *not* knowledge or power or
eternity, or anything else that the mind can grasp. God
is beyond all words and ideas.

The Wife Who Lost her Ring

One popular story of the Middle Ages was about a rich merchant whose wife began to spend a great deal of time in church. When her husband heard rumours that the church consisted of believers in the Free Spirit, he decided to follow her one day. Wearing a disguise, he walked behind her into an underground cavern where — to his surprise — the service began with a dance, in which everyone chose his or her partner. After that, the congregation ate food and drank wine. The husband began to understand why his wife preferred this to the local Catholic church; the service was better.

When the priest stood up, he announced that all human beings are free, and that provided they lived in the spirit of the Lord, they could do what they liked. "We must become one with God." Then he took a young girl and led her to the altar. The two of them removed their clothes. Then the priest turned to the congregation and told them to do the same. "This is the Virgin Mary and I am Jesus. Now do as we do." The girl lay down on the altar, and the priest lay on top of her and, in full view of the congregation, commenced an act of intercourse. Then the congregation each seized his dancing partner, and lay down on the floor.

In the chaos that followed, the wife did not notice as her husband took hold of her hand and pulled off her wedding ring; she was totally absorbed in her partner. Realizing that no one was paying any attention to him, the husband slipped away.

When his wife returned home, he asked her angrily how she dared to give herself to another man, even in the name of religion. She indignantly denied everything, demanding whether, as the wife of a wealthy merchant, he thought she would behave like a prostitute. But when the husband asked her what had happened to her wedding ring, she went pale. Then, as he held it out to her, she realized that he had seen everything, and burst into tears.

The wife was beaten until she bled, but she was more fortunate than the others, who were arrested by inquisitors and burnt at the stake.

The story may or may not have happened, but such congregations actually existed. They came into existence soon after the year AD 1200, and soon spread across Europe. The Free Spirit movement declared that God is within us all, and that therefore the Church is unnecessary — in fact, it is the Whore of Babylon. The great poets are as 'holy' as the Bible. Sex *must* be an acceptable way of worshipping God, since it brings such a sense of divine illumination. In his book *The Black Death*, Johanne Nohls gives this account of the Brethren:

"The bas reliefs . . . in French churches . . . represent erotic scenes. In the Cathedral of Alby a fresco even depicts sodomites engaged in sexual intercourse. Homosexuality was also well known in parts of Germany, as is proved by the trials of the Beghards and Beguins in the fourteenth century, particularly in the confessions of the brethren Johannes and Albert of Brünn, which are preserved in the Greifswald manuscript. From these it is evident that the Brethren of the Free Mind did not regard homosexuality as sinful. 'And if one brother desires to commit sodomy with a male, he should do so without let or hindrance and without any feeling of sin, as otherwise he would not be a Brother of the Free Mind.'"

In a Munich manuscript, we read: "And when they go to confession and come together and he preaches to them, he takes the one who is the most beautiful among them and does to her all according to his will, and they extinguish the light and fall one upon the other, a man upon a man, and a woman upon a woman, just as it comes about. Everyone must see with his own eyes how his wife or daughter is abused by others, for they assert that no one can commit sin below his girdle. That is their belief."

Other curious doctrines, "such as that incest is permissible, even when practised on the altar, that no one has the right to refuse consent, that Christ risen from the dead had intercourse with Magdalena, etc., all indicate the deterioration and confusion of moral ideas caused by the great plagues, particularly that of 1348"

In short, according to the Brethren of the Free Spirit, every man is his own messiah.

Sex with a Stranger

The Church did its best to stamp out these beliefs by sword and fire, but it still took three centuries. And even when the Free Spirits had been wiped out, the ideas continued to exert influence. Around 1550, a man named Klaus Ludwig, who lived in Mulhausen in Germany, formed a church in which members were initiated by having sex with a stranger. Like so many messiahs, Ludwig said he was Christ, the son of God, and that these things had been revealed to him. The sacrament was another name for sex. Man was bread and woman was wine, and when they made love, this was Holy Communion. Children born out such communion were holy. And the members of his congregation could not be killed. His sermons ended with the words "Be fruitful and multiply", and the congregation made haste to undress and do their best to obey.

Ludwig taught that sexual desire is the prompting of the Holy Spirit, so that if a man feels desire for any woman, he should regard it as a message from God. If, of course, the woman happened to be a member of Ludwig's "Chriesterung" (or Bloodfriends), then it was her duty to help him obey the will of the Lord, even if she was another man's wife.

Ludwig told the Bloodfriends to observe great secrecy and to behave like other people. But no doubt some of his congregation were eager to make converts of husbands with attractive wives. Like the congregation in the medieval story, the Bloodfriends were found out and put on trial, although Ludwig himself escaped. One member of the Council of Twelve Judges admitted that he had celebrated Holy Communion with sixteen different women. Three Bloodfriends were executed, and the others were re-converted to a more conventional form of Christianity.

Sabbatai Zevi

One of the most remarkable of all the "messiahs" was a Turkish Jew named Sabbatai Zevi (pronounced Shabtight Svy), who at one point seemed about to become one of the most powerful kings in Europe.

Sabbatai was the son of a wealthy merchant of Smyrna (now Izmir) on the coast of Turkey. Born in 1626, he was always of a deeply religious disposition; he spent hours in prayer, and at the age of sixteen, decided to observe a permanent fast, which lasted for six years. He permitted himself to be married to a girl whom his parents chose, but the marriage was never consummated, and she divorced him. The same thing happened to a second wife. He was what would nowadays be called a manic depressive, experiencing periods of immense joy and elation, followed by days of suicidal gloom.

In 1648, when Sabbatai was twenty-two a great tragedy occurred across the sea in Poland. The fierce Cossacks of the Ukraine rose against the Polish landlords. The Russians and

Poles had traditionally been enemies – in 1618 the Poles had even tried to put a Pole on the throne of Russia. The Russians and the Poles both wanted the rich Ukraine. A Cossack leader called Bogdan Khmelnitsky invaded Poland and challenged the Polish army. He also set out to destroy the Jews.

Poland's Jews had been servants of the rich landlords whom the Cossacks hated, and they were massacred in vast numbers. All the usual atrocities of massacre were committed – children hacked to pieces in their mothers' arms, pregnant women sliced open, old men disembowelled, girls raped before their husbands. One girl who had been forcibly married to a Cossack chose a cunning method of suicide: she told him that she had magic powers, and could not be harmed by a sword; if he didn't believe her, he should try running his sword through her. He did as she asked, and killed her.

A hundred thousand Jews died in this seventeenth century holocaust. Thousands of others fled the country, and many went to Turkey, where there were already wealthy Jewish communities.

When Sabbatai Zevi heard about these massacres he was appalled. Overwhelmed by a desperate desire to do something for his people, he suddenly became convinced he was the Messiah who would lead them back to the Holy Land. And he began his mission by doing something that horrified his orthodox fellow Jews – he stood up in the synagogue and pronounced the name of Jehovah (or Jahweh), which Jews regard as too sacred to speak. (Instead they called it Adonai.)

Like all messiahs, he soon collected a small band of followers who believed every word he said. His fellow orthodox Jews found this menacing, and banished him when he was twenty-five. In the Turkish town of Salonika (now Thessaloniki, and a part of Greece) he gained even more converts. But even his followers were often puzzled by his strange behaviour. On one occasion he went around carrying a basket of fish, explaining that it represented the Age of Pisces, when Jews would be released from bondage. And on another occasion he shocked the rabbis by inviting them to a feast, then taking a Scroll of the Law in his arms as if it were a woman, and carrying it to a marriage canopy that he had set up; this symbolic marriage of the Messiah and the Law shocked the orthodox so much that he was expelled from Salonika.

At the age of thirty-six, surrounded by disciples (who supported him in style) he moved to Jerusalem. There he was seen by a young man who was to become his John the Baptist or St Paul, the son of a Jewish scholar named Nathan Ashkenazi, who was deeply impressed when he saw Sabbatai in the street, but was too young and shy to approach him. It was at this time that Sabbatai found himself a bride, a Polish girl named Sarah, who had escaped the pogrom, become a courtesan (or high class tart), and developed a strange conviction that she was destined to be the bride of the Messiah. The story has it that Sabbatai heard about the beautiful courtesan and send twelve of his disciples to Leghorn, in Italy, to bring her to him. They were married in March 1664.

In the following year, Sabbatai finally met Nathan, who was now twenty-two (Sabbatai was nearly forty), and allowed himself to be convinced that it was time to announce to the whole world — and not merely to his disciples — that he was the Messiah.

The news spread throughout Palestine. But when Sabbatai rode seven times around the city of Jerusalem, then went to present himself to the rabbis as their new master, he met with violent hostility, and another order of banishment. Sabbatai now decided to return to the city of his birth, Smyrna. Meanwhile, his St Paul was writing letters to Jewish communities all over Europe announcing that the Messiah had come. These letters were read aloud in synagogues, and thousands of Jews were suddenly filled with hope that the Day of Judgement had at last arrived. In Amsterdam, another Jewish centre crowds danced in the streets. In London, Samuel Pepys recorded that Jews were placing ten to one bets that Sabbatai would soon be acknowledged as the King of the World.

Not all Jews shared this enthusiasm; the orthodox were appalled, for the doctinres preached by Sabbatai were horribly similar to those preached by the Brethren of the Free Spirit. "The forbidden" was now allowed, which included incest and promiscuity. The Sabbataians (as they were called) shocked their neighbours by walking around naked at a time when nakedness was regarded as a sin. In the Jewish religion, as in Mohammedanism, women were kept strictly apart. Sabbatai told them they were men's equals and should mix freely with their fellow worshippers. Divorce or infidelity was no reason for a woman to be excluded from full participation in religious rites. Was not the Messiah himself married to a woman who admitted to having been a whore?

Not that Sabbatai's followers were inclined to sexual self indulgence. They took pride in mortifying the flesh, scourging and starving themselves, rolling naked in the snow, even burying themselves in the earth so only their heads stuck out. It was a frenzy of religious ecstasy, all based on the belief that the Millennium was about to arrive.

Now Sabbatai made the mistake that was to dismay all his followers and bring an abrupt end to his career. He decided to go to Constantinople, the Turkish capital, a journey of fourteen days by sea. When the news reached Constantinople, it caused the same wild scenes of rejoicing that had been seen in other European capitals. There was a general feeling that the Day of Judgement was at hand, and that Sabbatai's arrival would finally restore the Jews to the glory they had enjoyed under King David.

There was a widespread belief in England in the late Middle Ages that the British were the descendants of Trojans who fled from Asia Minor after the fall of Troy. The Romans, in fact, believed that they were descendants of the Trojan prince Aeneas, who came to Italy after the fall of Troy. (Virgil described the wanderings of Aeneas after Troy in the *Aeneid*.)

Around AD 1140 Geoffrey of Monmouth published his immensely popular *History of the Kings of Britain*, which is largely about King Arthur and Merlin. But it begins by describing how Aeneas's great grandson Brutus (or Brute) was forced to flee from Italy after he accidentally killed his father when hunting. After various adventures, Brutus came to the island of Albion – inhabited then only by a few giants – and changed its name to Britain, after his own name. Geoffrey's book was accepted as reliable history even down to Elizabethan times.

The Sultan, the young Mehmet IV, was understandably alarmed. Enemies of Sabbatai informed his Grand Vizier, Ahmed Koprulu, that the Messiah was a charlatan who wanted the Sultan's throne. If Sabbatai had heard about this, he might have felt complimented. The people of Constantinople were prepared to welcome him as the people of Jerusalem had welcomed Jesus Christ, and the secular authorities thought he wanted to become king. History was repeating itself. His reply, of course, would be: "My kingdom is not of this world."

But the parallel with Jesus should also have warned him that he would soon be under arrest. In fact, the boat had only just docked – after a painful journey of thirty-six days – when Mehmet's soldiers came on board and carried him off to jail.

He was luckier than his messianic predecessor. Wealthy followers greased enough palms to make sure he was not put to death. Instead, he was installed in the castle of Abydos, in Gallipoli, and allowed to continue to live in style, with a succession of distinguished visitors. Unfortunately, one of these was a paranoid old man named Nehemiah ha-Kolen, a Polish scholar who wanted to argue with Sabbatai about the Kabbalah, the Jewish mystical system. He was determined to prove Sabbatai an imposter, or at least, compel him to acknowledge himself, Nehemiah, as an equal. Sabbatai stood up for himself, and probably allowed Nehemiah to see that he regarded him as a bilious and envious old neurotic. Nehemiah hastened away to denounce him to the Sultan as a revolutionary who had admitted that he hoped to usurp the throne. In September 1666, Sabbatai was brought before Sultan Mehmet, and ordered to convert to Islam or die on the spot. Faced with his supreme opportunity for martyrdom, Sabbatai behaved as unpredictably as ever. He promptly removed his Jewish skullcap and accepted a turban instead. He also accepted a new name: Azis Mehmet Effendi. His wife converted too, becoming known as Fatima Radini. The Sultan then granted him a comfortable sinecure as keeper of the palace gates, which carried a generous pension.

Sabbatai, it seemed, had simply abandoned his conviction that he was sent to save the world. He chose comfort – even though he secretly continued to practice Judaism. In public he was a good Mohammedan. But his followers knew better: they realized that this was another of his inexplicable actions.

Unfortunately, he was still subject to these extraordinary swings of mood, in one of which he divorced Sarah –

although he took her back again as soon as he was normal. And he also continued to preach sexual freedom. In due course, these views caused the Sultan embarrassment, and six years after his conversion, Sabbatai was arrested again. This time he was banished to a remote village in Albania, Dulcigno, where he lived on for another four years. Sarah predeceased him in 1674, and he married again. He still had manic moods in which he declared he was the Messiah, but no one paid any attention.

Oddly enough, his "John the Baptist", Nathan Ashkenazi, continued to love and revere him as the Messiah, as did thousands of followers, who regarded his conversion as yet another of his strange god-like actions — rather like those of the Japanese Zen masters who suddenly kick a pupil downstairs. Sabbatai was the only messiah known to history who was able to have it both ways — to proclaim himself a charlatan, and still continue to retain the devotion of his followers. He was the last of the great Jewish Messiahs.

These are only a small cross-section of the messiahs who have appeared since the crucifixion of Jesus of Nazareth. Readers who want a fuller account should read read Jack Gratus's *The False Messiahs* or Norman Cohn's *The Pursuit of the Millennium*, where they will find a wide array of amazing and colourful figures. This chapter, unfortunately, has run out of space.

Chapter Three

Tales of Bloodshed

We have seen that religious fanatics are capable of ruthless cruelty. But one notable figure of the thirteenth century could also be regarded as the father of modern terrorism. His name was Hasan bin Sabbah, and he is responsible for the modern word "assassin".

The Assassins

In the year 1273, the Venetian traveller Marco Polo passed through the valley of Alamut, in Persia, and saw there the castle of the Old Man of the Mountain, the head of the Persian branch of the sect of Ismailis, or Assassins. By that time, the sect was two hundred years old, and was on the point of being destroyed by the Mongols, who had invaded the Middle East under the leadership of Genghis Khan.

According to Marco Polo, the Old Man of the Mountain, whose name was Aloadin, had created a Garden of Paradise in a green valley behind the castle, and filled it with "pavilions and palaces the most elegant that can be imagined", fountains flowing with wine, milk and honey, beautiful *houris* who could sing and dance seductively. The purpose of this Garden was to give his followers a foretaste of Paradise, so that they might be eager to sacrifice their lives for their leader. When the Old Man wanted an enemy murdered, he would ask for volunteers. These men would be drugged and carried into the secret garden — which, under normal circumstances, was strictly forbidden to all males. They would awake to find themselves apparently in Paradise, with wine, food and damsels at their disposal. After a few days of this, they were again drugged and taken back to the Old Man's fortress. "So when the Old Man would have any prince slain, he would say to such a youth: 'Go thou and slay so-and-so; and when thou returnest, my angels shall bear thee to Paradise . . .'."

There is evidence that the story may have a foundation in fact. Behind the remains of the castle, which still exists in the valley of Alamut, there is a green enclosed valley with a spring. But it is hardly large enough to have contained "pavilions and palaces".

The Ismailis were a breakaway sect from the orthodox Moslems; they were the Mohammedan equivalent of Protestants. After the death of the prophet Mahomet in 632, his disciple Abu Bakr was chosen to succeed him, thus becoming the first Caliph of Islam. It is a pity that Mahomet, unlike Jesus, never made clear which of his disciples — or relatives — was to be the rock upon which his church was to be built. For other Moslems felt that the Prophet's cousin Ali was a more suitable candidate: the result was a dissension that split the Moslem world for centuries. The Sunni — the orthodox Moslems — persecuted and slaughtered Ali's followers, who were known as the Shi'a. In 680, they almost succeeded in wiping out their rivals, when seventy of them — including the prophet's daughter Fatima — were surprised and massacred. But the killers overlooked a sick boy — the son of Fatima; so the rebel tradition lived on.

All this murder and suffering produced powerful religious emotions among the Shi'a. They set up their own Caliph — known as the Imam — and they looked forward to the coming of a messiah (or Mahdi) who would lead them to final victory. Strange sects proliferated, led by holy men who came out of the desert. Some believed in reincarnation,

Two Assassins being instructed by the "Old Man of the Mountains".

others in total moral and sexual freedom. One sect believed in murder as a religious duty, strangling their victims with cords; these may be regarded as the true predecessors of the Assassins.

The Ismailis were a breakaway sect from the original breakaway sect. When the sixth Imam died, his eldest son Ismail was passed over for some reason, and his younger brother Musa appointed. The Ismailis were Moslems who declared that Ismail was the true Imam: they were also known as Seveners, because they believed that Ismail was the seventh and last Imam. The rest of the Shi'a became known as the Twelvers, for they accepted Musa and his five successors as true Imams. (The line came to an end after the twelfth.) The Twelvers became the respectable branch of the heretics, differing from orthodox Sunni only on a few points of doctrine. It was the Ismailis who became the true

53

opposition, creating a brilliant and powerful organization with its own philosophy, ritual and literature. They were intellectuals and mystics and fanatics. With such drive and idealism they were bound to come to power eventually.

It was some time around the middle of the eleventh century that the greatest of the Ismaili leaders was born – Hasan bin Sabbah, a man who combined the religious fervour of Saint Augustine with the political astuteness of Lenin. He founded the Order of Assassins, and became the first Old Man of the Mountain.

By the time Hasan was born, the Ismailis had become one of the great political powers. The Sunni Caliphs were decadent: the Ismailis set up their own Caliph and their own dynasty. They called themselves the Fatimids (descendants of Fatima, the Prophet's murdered daughter). They conquered the Nile valley, then spread slowly across Egypt, Syria, North Africa, parts of Arabia, even Sicily. By the end of the tenth century, it looked as if nothing could stop them becoming rulers of all the Moslem lands. But at that point, a new force entered Middle Eastern politics – the Seljuk Turks – who swept across the Moslem world like the ancient Romans. And the Turks, as good Moslems, decided to lend their support to the Sunni Caliphs. By the time Hasan bin Sabbah was a young man, the Ismaili empire was already past its peak.

Hasan was born an orthodox Moslem – or at least, a Twelver, which was almost the same thing. His family lived in Rayy, near modern Teheran. We know little about his early life except that he became an avid student of every branch of learning. A strong religious impulse led him to look beyond the sect into which he had been born. He was impressed by the intellectual force and mystical fervour of the heretical Ismailis. It took him a long time to decide to join them – for the Ismailis were generally regarded as outcasts and cranks. A serious illness decided him; in 1072 he took the oath of allegiance to the Fatimid Caliph. Four

In 1975 three of the islands in the Comoro group, which lies between Africa and Madagascar, declared their independence from France. Soon afterwards a man named Ali Soilih declared himself dictator of the tiny state with the military help of a French mercenary, Bob Denard. Soilih proved to be a despot: he raised death squads, kidnapped and raped women and organized the destruction of all machinery on the islands.

Two years into his reign, Soilih consulted a witch-doctor in order to know what the future held for himself and his descendants. The witch-doctor was encouraging: Soilih could only be killed by a man who owned a dog. Upon hearing this, Soilih acted as any dictator would and had his death squads kill all the dogs on the island.

Nevertheless, a year later he was dead, "shot while trying to escape" by the forces of his old comrade Bob Denard. The French mercenary had received a new contract, this time from one of Soilih's many enemies. And the witch-doctor had been right: among Denard's troops was his ever-present mascot, a large Alsatian dog.

Sunday Times

years later he was forced to leave Rayy — no doubt for spreading Ismaili doctrines — and started to make his way towards Cairo, a new city that had been built by the Ismailis as their capital. The journey took two years. In Cairo, he impressed the Caliph, and became a supporter of his eldest son Nizar. He spent three years in the Fatimid court; then his ardent revolutionary temperament got him into trouble

– history does not go into detail – and he left Egypt and became a wandering missionary for the Ismaili cause. Legend has it that he was sentenced to death, but that just before his execution, one of the strongest towers in the city collapsed suddenly; this was seen as an omen, so he was sent into exile instead. Another story tells how the ship on which he sailed ran into a violent storm; while the other passengers flung themselves on their knees and prayed, Hasan stood perfectly calm, explaining that he could not die until he had fulfilled his destiny. When the storm suddenly ceased, Hasan got the credit, and made several converts. "Thus," says Von Hammer (a thoroughly hostile chronicler), "to increase his credit, did he avail himself of accidents and natural occurrences, as if he possessed the command of both." Von Hammer seems to regard Hasan as a kind of Rasputin figure, a trickster and a fraud who used religion to gain personal power (but then, he also describes the Ismaili religion as "mysteries of atheism and immorality").

Hasan bin Sabbah was a highly successful missionary, particularly among his own people of Daylam, a wild, independent race who loathed the Turks. The Daylamis had been among the last to be converted to Islam, and even now they tended to be rebellious and unorthodox. Hasan saw their value. Their country was an ideal stronghold. And if Nizar failed to become the next Fatimid Caliph – which seemed highly likely, in view of the intrigues at court – Hasan might well need a stronghold.

As the number of his converts increased, Hasan selected his fortress, the castle of Alamut (or Eagle's Nest), perched high on a rock in the Elburz mountains, above a cultivated valley about thirty miles long.

His method of acquiring the castle was typical of his methods. First he sent "dais" – preachers – to the villages around the castle, and they made many converts. Then the dais got into the castle, and converted some of its garrison. The castle's owner, Alid – an orthodox Moslem – was not

The Assassins' Garden of Paradise.

sure what to do about all this. He seems to have been an indecisive man. At first he professed to be converted; then, one day, he persuaded the Ismailis to leave the castle, and slammed the gates. But he allowed himself to be persuaded to let them in again. At this point, Hasan was smuggled into the castle in disguise. One morning, Alid woke up to discover that his castle was no longer his own. He was politely shown the door and (according to one chronicler) given 3,000 gold dinars in compensation.

This was in 1090. From that time on, until his death thirty-five years later, Hasan lived in his castle. He studied, wrote books, brought up a family and planned conquests. Most of his followers never saw him. The religious rule in the castle was strict; they ate sparingly, and wine was forbidden. Hasan had one of his sons executed for drinking wine. (Another was executed on suspicion — false, as it later turned out — of having planned the murder of one of the dais.)

Cults and Fanatics

But if the aims were religious, the method was military. The Ismailis wanted to supplant the Sunni Caliphs of Baghdad. In order to do that, they first had to drive out the Turks who supported them. The Turks were the overlords of Persia. So Hasan's task was to extend his realm, village by village and castle by castle, until he could challenge the Turks directly. Where castles declined to be converted to the Ismaili faith, they were infiltrated or stormed. In towns and villages, Ismaili converts rose up and took control. Like T. E. Lawrence – in his own battle to overthrow the Turks – Hasan's great advantage was the hatred of the conquered people for their overlords. When he had extended his control to all the area surrounding Alamut, he sent a missionary to the mountainous country called Quhistan in the southeast, where various heretical sects were oppressed by the Turks. There was a popular rising, the Turks were overthrown, and Quhistan became the second great Ismaili stronghold. Not long after, another area of mountain country in the southwest became an Ismaili stronghold when another of Hasan's followers seized two castles near Arrajan. The Turks now became aware of their danger, and decided it was time to crush the Ismailis; two great expeditions were sent out, one against Alamut, the other against Quhistan. They soon discovered how well Hasan had chosen his fortresses. Although there were a mere seventy defenders, the castle of Alamut was impregnable to direct attack; and the surrounding villages made sure the defenders were not starved into submission by smuggling food up to them by night. A surprise attack sent the Turkish armies flying. The expedition against Quhistan fared no better.

And it was at this point, in 1092, a mere two years after moving to Alamut, that Hasan made the great decision that may well have been his crucial mistake. He recognized that open war with the Turks was out of the question; his armies were too small. But his followers were fanatics who would give their lives for their cause. Why not use them to strike down his chief enemies, one by one? In 1092, the "assassins" claimed their first, and perhaps their most eminent victim, Nizam Al-Mulk, the Vizier of the Turkish Sultan.

Until recent years, it was accepted that Nizam Al-Mulk had been a fellow student of Hasan's. The story told by Von Hammer — who repeats it from earlier Persian chroniclers — is that Hasan, Nizam Al-Mulk and the poet Omar Khayyam were fellow students, and Hasan suggested to the other two that if any of them should achieve eminence, he should share it with the other two. They all agreed. After some years, Nizam became the Vizier of the Turkish Sultan Alp Arslan, one of the great military geniuses of the period. When Alp Arslan died (1073) and his young son, Malik Shah, came to the throne, Nizam became the most powerful man in the land. At this point, his old schoolfellows presented themselves and reminded him of their agreement. Omar, being a poet and mathematician (one of the greatest of the Middle Ages), asked only for a quiet place to study; so Nizam gave him a pension and sent him back to his home town of Naishapur. Hasan wanted power, so Nizam found him a position at court. What happened then is not quite clear, except that Nizam realized that his old schoolfellow was supplanting him in the royal favour, and took steps to bring about his downfall. Hasan left Malik's court vowing vengeance; and that, says Von Hammer, is why Nizam became the first victim of the Assassins.

By 1092, Nizam Al-Mulk was Hasan's chief enemy, the greatest single danger to the Assassins. Hasan asked for a volunteer to kill the Vizier. A man called Bu Tahir Arrani stepped forward. He disguised himself as a Sufi — a holy man — and during the feast of Ramadan, in October, 1092, was allowed to approach the litter of Nizam as he was carried out of his audience tent. He drove a knife into Nizam's breast, and was himself immediately killed by Nizam's guards. When he heard that the assassination had been successful, Hasan remarked: "The killing of this devil is the beginning of bliss." He meant it literally; his followers accepted that to die like Bu Tahir Arrani was an immediate passport to Paradise.

It may be that this murder showed Hasan where his real power lay. He could capture a fortress by preaching, cunning and bribery. He could destroy an enemy by sending out a single assassin. It looked like the ideal formula for guerrilla warfare.

Where he made his mistake was in failing to grasp the ultimate consequences of such a method: that if his men destroyed their enemies like scorpions or cobras, they would arouse the same loathing and detestation as scorpions or cobras. And that sooner or later, the horror they inspired would cancel all their gains. It was this that eventually frustrated Hasan's plans for conquest.

But that lay far in the future. For the moment, Hasan's method was triumphantly successful. Not long after Nizam's death, the Sultan Malik also died — of a stomach complaint, apparently. One of Nizam's sons, Fakhri, was killed in Naishapur; he had been accosted by a beggar who said: "The true Moslems are no more and there are none left to take the hand of the afflicted." As Fakhri reached for alms, he was stabbed to the heart. Nizam's other son, Ahmed, laid siege to the castle of Alamut; the inhabitants suffered severe hardships, but again it proved impregnable. Ahmed was later stabbed by an assassin, but he recovered.

The candidates for assassination were always carefully chosen. Hasan played his game like a master chess player. The death of Malik Shah brought on a struggle for power at court; the new Sultan, Berkyaruq, had to defend his throne against his half-brothers. Hasan lent his support to Berkyaruq, and assassinated a number of Berkyaruq's enemies. Berkyaruq's officers formed an uneasy liaison with the Assassins. So when Berkyaruq finally put down the rebellion, Hasan was allowed to operate in peace for a few years.

But he continued to practise the arts of infiltration and intimidation; Ismailis joined Berkyaruq's army, and made converts. When officers opposed them, they were silenced with the threat of assassination. A point came where no one in authority dared to go out without armour under his robes. Leaders of rival religious sects were murdered. One opponent was stabbed in the mosque as he knelt at prayers, even though a bodyguard was standing directly behind him. Eventually – in 1101 – Berkyaruq lost his temper and decided it was time to destroy the Ismailis. He combined with his half-brother Sanjar to attack the stronghold at Quhistan; the armies laid waste the countryside, destroying the crops, and would have captured the main stronghold (Tabas) if the Ismailis had not bribed the enemy general to go away – a typically oriental touch. Sanjar made other attempts to subjugate the Ismailis, but eventually came to tolerate them. The historian Juvanyi tells a story to explain this. Hasan managed to bribe one of Sanjar's guards to stick a dagger into the ground near his head, when Sanjar lay in a drunken sleep. Shortly thereafter, Sanjar received a message from Hasan that said: "That dagger could just as easily have been stuck in your heart." Sanjar saw the wisdom of tolerating the Ismailis.

Nevertheless, Hasan's dreams began to collapse within a few years of his greatest triumphs. In 1094, the Fatimid Caliph – spiritual head of the Ismailis – died in Cairo. Nizar – Hasan's patron – should have replaced him. Instead, the Vizier, Al-Afdal, put Nizar's younger brother on the throne. There was a war, and Nizar was killed. Hasan remained faithful to Nizar (in fact, his sect called themselves the Nizari); he refused to acknowledge the new Sultan. So he was now isolated from his own co-religionists. After Berkyaruq turned against him, it was all the Assassins could do to hold on to their territories. At eighty-seven, he was getting tired; he could not afford to defy the whole Arab world forever. But before the Caliph and the Old Man of the Mountain could make peace, the new Vizier discovered a plot by the Assassins to murder the Caliph. In all probability, there was never such a plot. Nizar and his children were dead; Hasan had no motive for wanting to kill the man who was now offering him peace and cooperation. But the Vizier was a Twelver (not an Ismaili); he had good reason for wanting to prevent the reconciliation. And Hasan's reputation was such that any mud would stick. The Caliph took the "plot" so seriously that he ordered that all the citizens of Cairo should be registered, and that all strangers should be carefully watched. Many "agents of Hasan" were arrested and executed, including the tutor of the Caliph's children.

And so the last hope vanished. And in May 1144, Hasan bin Sabbah, one of the most remarkable religious leaders of all time, died in his castle of Alamut, at the age of ninety. He appointed one of his generals to succeed him, demonstrating thereby that he had learned from Mahomet's chief mistake.

This was by no means the end of the Assassins. After initial difficulties, the Syrian branch took root, and it was the stories of the Syrian mission, carried back to Europe by Crusaders, that introduced the word "assassin" into the European languages. The event that caused this notoriety was the murder of the Christian Knight Conrad of Montferrat in 1192; Conrad was stabbed by two Assassins – agents of the Syrian Old Man of the Mountain, Sinan – who were disguised as monks. (King Richard the Lion Heart of England is supposed to have been behind the murder; one of his protégés quickly married the widow, and became "King of Jerusalem" in his place.) After this, Assassins began to figure in every chronicle of the Third Crusade, and the legend captured the imagination of Europe. They were masters of disguise, adepts in treachery and murder. Their Old Man was a magician who surveyed the world from his castle like some evil spider, watching for victims. They were without religion and without morality (one early chronicler says they ate pork — against the Moslem law — and practised incest with their mothers and sisters). They were so fanatically devoted to their master that he often demonstrated their obedience to visitors by making them leap out of high windows. Their arts of persuasion were so subtle that no ruler could be sure of the loyalty of his own servants . . . A typical story illustrates this. Saladin — the Sultan of Egypt and the great enemy of the Crusaders — sent a threatening message to Sinan, the Syrian Old Man. The Assassin chief sent back a messenger, whose mission was to deliver a message in private. Aware of the danger, Saladin had him thoroughly searched, then dismissed the assembly, all except for two guards. The messenger turned to the guards and asked: "If I were to order you, in the name of my Master, to kill the Sultan, would you do it?" They nodded and drew their swords. Whereupon the messenger, having made his point, bowed and took his leave — taking the two guards with him. Saladin decided to establish friendly relations with the Assassins . . .

But by the time Marco Polo saw the castle of Alamut in 1273, the power of the Assassins was at an end. In Persia they had been slaughtered by the Mongols; in Syria, ruthlessly suppressed by Baybars, Sultan of Egypt. Some of the survivors remained in the area of Alamut — where they may be found to this day. Others scattered to distant countries, including India . . .

The Thugs

By AD 1300, the Assassins had ceased to exist in the Middle East, at least as a political force. In 1825, the English traveller J. B. Fraser, remarked that although the Ismailis no longer committed murder, they were still fanatically devoted to their chief. Fraser also commented that there were Ismailis in India too. This raises a fascinating question: whether the Assassins of the Middle East formed a liaison with their Indian counterparts, the Thugs. When William Sleeman was investigating the Thugs in the nineteenth century, he was puzzled why, although they were Moslems, they worshipped the Hindu goddess Kali. One captured Thug explained that Kali was identical with Fatima, the murdered daughter of the prophet . . .

The Thugs (pronounced "tug") came to the attention of Europe after the British annexation of India in the late eighteenth century. At first, the conquerors noted simply that the roads of India seemed to be infested with bands of robbers who strangled their victims. In 1816, a doctor named Robert Sherwood, stationed in Madras, induced some of these robbers to talk to him about their religion. His article "On the Murderers Called Phansigars" appeared in *Asiatic Researches* in 1820, and caused some excitement. Sherwood alleged that the phansigars or Thugs (phansi means a noose; thug means cheat) committed murders as a religious duty, and that their aim was the actual killing, rather than the robbery that accompanied it.

The bizarre story caught the imagination of the English, and the word "thug" soon passed into the language. The Thugs, according to Sherwood, lived quietly in their native villages for most of the year, fulfilling their duties as citizens and fathers in a manner that aroused no suspicion. But in the month of pilgrimage (usually November-December) they took to the roads and slaughtered travellers – always taking care to be at least a hundred miles from home.

The method was always the same. The advance guard would locate a band of travellers, then one or two of the Thugs would approach the group and ask if they might travel with it – for protection. A few days later, a few more Thugs would make the same request. This would continue until there were more Thugs than travellers. The killing usually took place in the evening, when the travellers were seated around the fire. At a given signal, three Thugs would take their place behind each victim. One of them would pass the strangling cloth (or *ruhmal*) around the victim's neck; another would grab his legs and lift them clear of the ground; the third would seize his hands or kneel on his back. Usually, it was all over within seconds. The bodies of the victims were then hacked and mutilated to prevent recognition, and to make them decompose more quickly. The legs were cut off; if there was time, the whole body might be dismembered. Then it was buried. It was now time for the most important part of the ritual – the ceremony known as *Tuponee*. A tent was usually erected – to shield the Thugs from the sight of travellers. The *kussee*, the consecrated pickaxe (their equivalent of the Christian cross), was placed near the grave: the Thugs sat around in a group. The leader prayed to Kali for wealth and success. A symbolic strangling was enacted, and then all who had taken an active part in the murder ate the "communion sugar" (*goor*), while the chief poured consecrated water on the grave. One of the captured Thugs told Sleeman: "Let any man once taste of that *goor* and he will be a Thug, though he know all the trades and have all the wealth of the world."

William Sleeman was a captain in the British army; born in St Tudy, Cornwall, he had served in India since 1809. He was fascinated by Sherwood's paper, and in the early 1820s, he began to study the Thugs in the Nerbudda Valley. The revelations he made in 1829 caused a sensation throughout India. Sleeman revealed that Thuggee was not a local religious sect, but a nationwide phenomenon that claimed the lives of thousands of travellers every year. Sleeman became the acknowledged authority on the subject, and in 1830, Lord William Bentinck appointed him to suppress the Thugs.

Fortunately for Sleeman, the organization had already become corrupt and degenerate. In its earlier days, the members of the sect had been strict in their observance of the rules. It was forbidden to kill women, because Kali was a woman; it was also forbidden to kill religious mendicants, carpenters, metal workers, blind men, pariahs, lepers, mutilated men, and men driving a goat or cow. Greed had caused a gradual relaxation of the rules (it must have been infuriating to let a rich caravan escape because it contained a carpenter or blind man); and it was to this disobedience that the Thugs attributed their decline in fortunes. In a sense, this was true. Haste and greed meant that bodies were sometimes left unburied, so a search could be instituted more quickly. And in some cases, lack of preparation meant that the killing was bungled – Sleeman mentions a case in which the Thugs were pursued back to their own village, and saved from arrest only by the intervention of the villagers (who had been well bribed). When Sleeman's researches were published, travellers became suspicious of "holy men" or poor Moslems who asked for protection. Better roads (built by the British) meant that Thugs could be pursued more easily. Many of them became informers (or "approvers") to save their own lives. Within a few years, thousands of Thugs had been arrested and brought to trial.

Sleeman was the first to understand the fundamentally religious nature of Thuggee: that the murders were sacrifices offered to the dark mother, Kali (also known as Durgha and Bhowani). Because he was deeply religious, the Thug was usually scrupulous, honest, kindly and trustworthy; Sleeman's assistant described one Thug chief as "the best man I have ever known". Many Thugs were rich men who held responsible positions; part of their spoils went to local Rajahs or officials, who had no objection to Thugs provided they committed their murders elsewhere. Colonel James Sleeman, grandson of Sir William, described Feringheea as "the Beau Nash of Thuggee". Like the Assassins, most convicted Thugs met their deaths with remarkable bravery, which impressed their British executioners. It is this Jekyll and Hyde character that makes the Thugs so baffling. One old Thug was the nurse of a family of British children, and obviously regarded his charges with great tenderness; for precisely one month of every year he obtained leave to visit his "sick mother"; the family found it unbelievable when he was arrested as a Thug. For the Thugs were capable of murdering children as casually as adults. A Thug leader described how his gang decoyed a group of twenty-seven – including five women and two children – away from a larger group of travellers (arguing that they could travel more cheaply). At midnight they stopped to rest in a grove – already chosen in advance as the murder place. There the Thugs strangled the adults; the children – two three-year-old boys – were given to two Thugs; but one of them kept crying for his mother, whom he had just seen murdered. The Thug picked him up by his feet and dashed out his brains against a rock. This was one of the few occasions when retribution followed. The adults were buried, but the Thugs overlooked the boy's body. It was discovered the next morning by the local landowner, who set out to hunt the Thugs with armed men. After a chase, the Thugs were located; when the armed men opened fire, they scattered, leaving behind much of their booty. Four thugs were arrested, and kept in captivity for a few years. (Sleeman points out that the landowner's motive was not a sense of justice, but to seize the spoils.) The other boy was brought up as a Thug.

The male children of Thugs were automatically initiated into the sect. They were first placed in the care of a Thug tutor, who insisted upon absolute obedience, and acted as their religious instructor. (It must be emphasized that the killing was only a part of the ritual of the Thugs, as Communion is of Christians.) At the age of nine or ten, the boys were allowed to act as scouts, and later to watch the killing. At eighteen they were allowed to take part in the killing and eat the *goor*.

Cults and Fanatics

By the year 1850, Thuggee had virtually ceased to exist in India. Over 4,000 Thugs had been brought to trial; some were hanged, others sentenced to transportation or life imprisonment. Sleeman came to know many of them – even to establish a kind of friendship; for example, he was instrumental in getting the notorious Feringheea a pardon (in the face of some opposition, for when the Thug leader was caught, he admitted that he had just returned from an expedition in which 105 men and women had died).

The mystery of the origin of Thuggee is still unsolved. Feringheea told Sleeman that all the Thug rituals were portrayed in the eighth-century carvings in the caves of Ellora. (Ellora is a village in northeast Bombay province, and its Hindu, Buddhist and Jain temples extend for over a mile, with some of India's greatest sculptural treasures, whose dates range from the third to the thirteenth century.) If this is true, then the Thugs pre-dated the Assassins by three hundred years. In his book *The Assassins*, Bernard Lewis suggests that the Thugs may have been connected with the stranglers of Iraq – the heretical sect that sprang up after the death of the Prophet. But these stranglers flourished in the first half of the eighth century, and four more centuries were to elapse before the Moslems made deep inroads into India. (The greatest of the early Moslem invaders of India, Mahmud of Ghazni – Khayyam's "mighty Mahmud" – confined himself to the Punjab, in northwestern India: Delhi fell to Mohammed of Ghur in 1192.) So it is altogether more likely that Ismailis, fleeing from persecution after the fall of Alamut, discovered that India already possessed its own Order of Assassins, and formed an alliance with the Thugs.

The Median prophet Zoroaster who founded the ancient fire-worshipping religion of Persia, ate only cheese for thirty years of his life.

Other Ismailis formed their own sects in India, and continued to regard the Persian Imam as their head. In 1811, the French consul Rousseau observed that Ismailis flourished in India, and that they regarded their Imam almost as a god. In 1850, a sect of Ismailis known as the Khojas decided to settle a religious dispute by their old methods, and four dissenting brethren were assassinated in broad daylight. The four killers were hanged. The quarrel centred around the question of whether the Khojas of Bombay province still owed allegiance to the Persian Imam. This Imam was known as the Aga Khan; and a few years later, he was forced to flee to India — after an unsuccessful attempt to overthrow the Shah of Persia — and became the spiritual head of the Ismailis — not only in India, but also in Persia, Syria and central Asia. And so the homeland of the Thugs became eventually the homeland of the descendants of the Assassins.

To find a parallel to the fanaticism of the Assassins and the Thugs, we have to turn to some of the bizarre sects of Old Russia.

The Khlysty and the Skoptzy

In the section on Rasputin (*see page 25*), I have deliberately said nothing about the strange religious cult to which he belonged, for it would have led to a long digression. In fact, when the young Rasputin visited the monastery of Verkhoture with a novice called Mileti Saborevsky, he learned that it was also a kind of prison, a place of detention for certain members of heretical sects, the chief of which were the Khlysty, or Flagellants, and the Skoptzy, or Mutilators. During his four months in the monastery, Rasputin enjoyed speaking with these heretics, and he learned that the Khlysty believed that the Kingdom of God can only be attained on this earth by the Elect. They, of course, were the Elect.

He also learned that one of the reasons the Khlysty were so disliked by the Orthodox Church was that their ceremonies were regarded as scandalous and immoral. Since Rasputin was young and highly sexed, he probably felt that this was something that deserved looking into. At all events, he became a member of the Khlysty, and his enemies later declared that he had carried his beliefs back to his home in Pokrovskoe, and made them the excuse to seduce half the women in the village. There is undoubtedly an element of truth in this accusation.

But in order to understand the Khlysty, and their even stranger offshoot, the Skoptzy, we need to know a little about the great religious controversy that split Russia into two warring camps at about the same time that Sabbatai Zevi was causing so much ferment in the Middle East.

The man who was to blame was, in many ways, very like Grigory Rasputin.

Nikon Mordvinov was a peasant who turned to religion when his three children died. He made the acquaintance of the Tsar Alexis on a visit to Moscow in 1645, became a favourite, and was soon the most powerful man in Russia. He was appointed Patriarch in 1652, and while the Tsar was away at the wars, Nikon acted as his regent and governed Russia.

Nikon was a fanatic and a bully, and he decided to reform the church by force. Things were slack in the Russian church; the priest was usually regarded as of small importance, and could be ordered about by the village commune. Nikon treated the priests sternly; he ordered them to demand respect and obedience, and when he thought they were not fulfilling their duties, he had them tortured and imprisoned. He also decided to revise the service and prayer book of the Russian church. Some of these revisions sound absurd. He ordered a slight change in the spelling of "Jesus", and decreed that believers should cross themselves with three fingers instead of two. He also made many arbitrary changes in the prayer books — for example, changing "temple" to "church", and vice versa.

The violent resistance that he met was almost certainly not due to the changes he proposed, but to dislike of being bullied. Those who resisted him called themselves Old Believers. After twelve years, Nikon overreached himself and lost the Tsar's favour; his chief enemy, Avvakum, was recalled from a Siberian exile, and took Nikon's place as the Tsar's favourite. But the Old Believers had not won. The struggle went on with increased bitterness for the rest of the century. Huge numbers of Old Believers committed suicide — sometimes *en masse* by burning themselves on huge pyres. (Mussorgsky's opera *Khovantschina* ends with such a scene.)

Violent passions were aroused, but they were not necessarily religious passions. As in England at the same period, religion and politics were closely entangled. Still, there were many deaths, many mass executions, much cruelty, and the struggle produced convictions where they had not previously existed. As a result, Russia became a country in which religion was an important issue. While the old-fashioned Greek orthodoxy had prevailed, Russia was a country with only one form of Christianity. The schism in Russia produced the same effect as Luther's Reformation in Europe; new sects began to spring up overnight.

Two of these — and perhaps the most interesting — are closely related: the Khlysty and the Skoptzy, the Flagellants and the Mutilants.

It has been suggested that the Khlysty existed as long ago as 1363. This is possible, but it is certain that the great schism gave the sect a new vitality. The Khlysty have a certain amount in common with the ancient sect of the Manichees: they divide the world into spirit and flesh, and believe the spirit to be good, the flesh evil. But their most important characteristic is the belief that Christ keeps returning to earth as a man. The resurrection is understood in this sense. Christ's body remained in the tomb, but his spirit took another body, and has continued to do so throughout the ages. Averzhan was one of these Christs, and was crucified on the battlefield of Kulikovo in 1380 by Dmitri Donskoi. (Kulikovo is the Russian equivalent of the Battle of Hastings, when Dmitri defeated the Mongols.) Another Christ, Yemeljan, suffered under Ivan the Terrible, according to Karl Grass's *Russian Sects*. But the most important of the Christs was Daniel Philipov, who was a contemporary of Nikon. Philipov was a peasant from Kostroma who deserted the army and supported the cause of the Old Believers. The spirit of God descended on him one day when he stood on the hill of Golodina in the Volost of Starodub (in Vladimir), in the form of the god Zebaoth, who descended with a host of angels and entered Philipov's body. The Khlysty call this "the second advent". He began preaching in the village of Staraya, which in Khlysty mythology has the same kind of importance as Medina in Mohammedanism, and moved to Kostroma, which is the Khlysty Mecca. He produced a Bible called the Dove Book, and preached that men should not marry, should not drink or swear, and should look out for martyrdom. If one of his converts was married, he should abandon his wife, and his children should be called "sins". He was allowed to take a new "spiritual wife", a member of the Khlysty, who might sleep with him in the same bed as his old wife — but there should be no carnal relation.

The most frequently repeated story about the Khlysty concerns their method of worship. This was always held in the utmost secrecy. The celebrants were dressed in white, and danced around a fire or a tub of water, chanting their hymns. Yussupov's account of their practices declares:

They attained this heavenly communion by the most bestial practices, a monstrous combination of the Christian religion with pagan rites and primitive superstitions. The faithful used to assemble by night in a hut or forest clearing, lit by hundreds of tapers. The purpose of these *radenyi*, or ceremonies, was to create a religious ecstasy, an erotic frenzy. After invocations and hymns, the faithful formed a ring and began to sway in rhythm, then to whirl round and round, spinning faster and faster. As a state of dizziness was essential to the "divine flux", the master of ceremonies flogged any dancer whose vigour abated. The *radenyi* ended in a horrible orgy, everyone rolling on the ground in ecstasy or in convulsions. They preached that he who is possessed by the spirit belongs not to himself but to the spirit who controls him and who is responsible for all his actions and for any sins he may commit.

Finally the lights were blown out, and the worshippers coupled freely — the results, according to one writer, frequently being incestuous.

This is an interesting account, but it should not be taken too seriously. No doubt this kind of thing *did* occur, but it was not the rule. In his book *Russian Dissenters*, Frederick Conybeare gives a less sensational description.

The celebrants danced around the tub of water (which, he says, would begin to boil and give off a golden steam *of its own accord*) and flagellated one another, meanwhile chanting their hymns, many of them containing nonsense words that are supposed to be the utterance of the Holy Spirit. Some of them would have hallucinations and declare that a raven or a mother and child were rising from the vapours of the tub. They would finally collapse with exhaustion, and lie asleep for hours. No doubt these rites often led to orgies in the dark. They are reminiscent of the modern snake handling cults of southern America described by William Sargant in *Battle for the Mind*:

The descent of the Holy Ghost on these meetings, which were reserved for whites, was supposedly shown by the occurrence of wild excitement, bodily jerkings, and the final exhaustion and collapse, in the more susceptible participants. Such hysterical states were induced by means of rhythmic singing and hand-clapping, and the handling of genuinely poisonous snakes . . . brought several visitors unexpectedly to the point of collapse and sudden conversion. But a young male visitor . . . was attending these meetings with the deliberate object of seducing girls who had just been "saved". The fact is that . . . protective inhibition causes a breakdown and leaves the mind highly susceptible to new behaviour patterns . . .

No doubt a great deal of this kind of thing occurred with the Khlysty.

The Skoptzy were a development of the Khlysty, and should be mentioned here to complete the picture of the background of religious dissent in Russia. The Khlysty judged a man's "Christhood" by his ability to suffer bodily pain. Daniel Philipov was, according to tradition, crucified twice. Philipov's "spiritual son" and successor, Ivan Suslov, went one better, and was crucified three times (either at the order of Alexis or Peter the Great). He was also tortured by red-hot irons, and had his skin flayed off him. (On this occasion, a virgin managed to get hold of his skin, and handed it over to him when he rose from his third crucifixion.) Philipov died in 1700, ascending bodily to heaven. Suslov, who had carried his preaching to Moscow, and established his right to remain there by refusing to stay dead, died about three years later.

Seventy years later, an ancient lady called Akulina Ivanovna was known by the Khlysty as "the mother of God". It was she who recognized the "Christhood" of a man called Ivanov, who became reverenced under the name of

Kondrati Selivanov, and became the founder of the Skopt-zy. Selivanov went further in asceticism than the Khlysty, and declared that men should be castrated, and that women should have their breasts amputated and (if they could bear it) also have their genitals mutilated. In his early fifties, shortly after "the mother of God" had recognized him as her spiritual son, Selivanov emasculated himself with a red-hot-iron. (Later he declared that he had done this at fourteen; even his followers did not accept this estimate.) By this time, Catherine the Great was on the throne; she had murdered (or connived at the murder) of her husband, Peter the Third. This caused her some trouble, for Selivanov claimed to be Peter the Third. Later, a Don cossack, Pugachev, assumed the title and led a rebellion that was very nearly successful. Pugachev was finally caught and taken to Moscow in an iron cage, where he was executed with characteristic barbarity — his hands and feet were cut off and he was quartered alive. Again, in 1768, a Serbian adventurer successfully posed as Peter the Third and seized the principality of Montenegro in what is now Yugoslavia.

Selivanov's assumption of the title seems to have led to no violent repercussions; he was captured and placed in a mental home in the capital. When Alexander I came to the throne in 1801, he was released. By this time he had many disciples among the wealthy and influential, and he was allowed to conduct his "religion" openly. He wrote a book called *The Passion* which circulated widely, and he mutilated a hundred adults with his own hand. It was at this time that he actually changed his name from Ivanov to Selivanov. He continued to declare that he was Peter the Third, and his followers carried a coin with a picture of the sovereign on it (presumably it must have resembled Selivanov) and many kept pictures of the prince as an icon, and said their prayers in front of it. Selivanov lived until 1830, by which time he was well over a hundred years old. He had been interned in a monastery in Suzdal for the last ten years of his life, but this did not diminish his influence; his followers made it a place of pilgrimage. His followers — there were still many thousands of them at the time of the October revolution — believe that he will reappear in the neighbourhood of Irkutsk when the number of his followers reaches 144,000, and will inaugurate the day of Judgment. The 144,000 will have to be virgins, male and female. Children born into the sect grow up with the knowledge that they will be mutilated when they reach puberty, any who try to escape are hunted down and assassinated, according to Conybeare. Mutilation is not obligatory among women, but is apparently expected. Sometimes the removal of a nipple is regarded as sufficient.

Sacheverell Sitwell has written of the Skoptzy in his *Roumanian Journey*, and tells of a typical case that took place in 1868 (when Selivanov was generally believed to be still alive, although he had been dead for thirty-eight years). This took place in Tambov, and concerned a rich merchant called Plotitsine from Morshansk. Some of his servants were arrested for failure to pay taxes, and the merchant's frantic efforts to get them released aroused suspicion of the police, who investigated his house. It was discovered to be a colony of about forty Skoptzy, many of them described as "beautiful young girls". The men were flabby, with woman-like hips and high-pitched voices; the women who had suffered the operation (not all of them) were almost indistinguishable from the men. All were tried and sent to Siberia.

It might seem that the Skoptzy would at least escape the accusation of sexual orgies so often made against the Khlysty, but this is not so. It is reported that many of the women were mutilated only perfunctorily, and actually became prostitutes who earned money for the communal treasury. Many men performed the operation on themselves, and halted before they emasculated themselves. These Skoptzy were known as the Skoptzy of the Lesser

Seal, to distinguish them from the fully mutilated members of the Greater Seal. It is therefore possible that the accusations of sexual orgies made against the Skoptzy may have a foundation in fact.

The Khlysty and the Skoptzy would not be the only strange sects that Rasputin probably encountered on his journeys through Russia. There was a sect of Ticklers, in which the men tickled the women to induce religious ecstasy; sometimes the tickling resulted in a state of exhaustion that ended in death, and those who died were regarded as lucky at having achieved salvation.

In his book *The Sacred Fire*, B.Z. Goldberg mentions various suicide sects which seem to be related to the Skoptzy. In the reign of Alexander the Second, a man named Shodkin founded such a sect, and led his followers into a cave, which they proceeded to seal up. Two women became panic stricken and broke out. Shodkin then called upon his followers to kill one another before the police arrived. The children were murdered first, then the women; when the police arrived, only Shodkin and two of his acolytes were alive.

Chapter Four

More Massacres

The Black Death and the Flagellants

In AD 1345, a horrible disease called the Black Death began to develop among the corpses of earthquake and flood victims in China, and was carried by rats along the caravan trails to Europe. It reached the Crimea, in southern Russia, in 1346. In a manner that seems sadly typical of human nature, the Tartars looked around for a scapegoat, and decided that the Christians must be to blame. They chased the Genoese merchants to their fortified town of Caffa, then surrounded it and began to bombard it. But the plague had followed them, and the beseigers were soon dying in an agony of thirst, with swellings in the groins and armpits, and the black spots on the skin which gave the disease its name.

Before they left, the Tartars decided to give the Christians a taste of the misery they were suffering, and used giant catapults to lob plague-ridden corpses over the walls. The merchants carried them immediately to the sea, but they were too late. The Black Death took a grip in the town, and soon the merchants decided to flee back to Europe. They took the Black Death with them. It quickly spread from Messina, the Sicilian port where the merchants landed, as far as England, killing approximately half the population.

Again there was a search for scapegoats. In Germany, it was rumoured that Jews had been poisoning the wells, and fleeing Jews were seized at Chillon and tortured. Under torture, they confessed to the charge. They were executed, and there were massacres of Jews in Provence, at Narbonne and Carcassone, then all over Germany: Strasbourg, Frankfurt, Mainz and the

Flagellants in medieval Germany.

trading towns of the north belonging to the Hanseatic League. Here Jews were walled in their houses and left to starve; others were burnt alive.

Another scapegoat was the leper. In the Middle Ages, lepers were usually regarded with considerable tolerance and allowed to form grimly picturesque processions; now they were stoned to death, or simply refused entry into the walled towns.

One of the stranger phenomena that flourished under the Black Death was the movement known as Flagellants. These had originated about a century earlier in Italy, when various plagues and famines convinced the Italians that God wanted them to show repentance, and took the form of pilgrimages in which people walked naked to the waist, beating themselves

79

New York's "Son of Sam" serial killer David Berkowitz claimed at his trial to have been driven to kill by "demon voices" in his head. After he was found guilty and sentenced, he held a press conference to say that his claims of demonic possession were untrue, being calculated to produce a lenient punishment. Yet evidence that Berkowitz *was* part of a Satanic cult that ordered him to kill, and indeed may have committed some of the killings attributed to him, came to light after he was caught.

In one of his anonymous letters to NYPD Berkowitz had mentioned: "John 'Wheaties' rapist and suffocator of young girls". An investigative journalist named Maury Terry found out that "Wheaties" had been the nickname of one of Berkowitz' associates, John Carr. After much work Terry traced Carr. He was dead, shot in the mouth with a shotgun. The police reached the conclusion that it was suicide despite the letters S.S.N.Y.C. being written in blood on the wall next to the body. Terry discovered that Berkowitz and Carr had both gone to Satanic meetings in Yonkers, New York, an area where eighty-five skinned dogs had been found over the year before the killings started. Berkowitz also showed knowledge of ritualistic killings that had received very little news coverage. He wrote in a letter to a preacher in California: ". . . I was a member of an occult group. Being sworn to secrecy or face death, I cannot reveal the name of this group . . . It was (and still is) blood oriented. These people will stop at nothing, including murder."

A procession of flagellants.

with whips or scourges tipped with metal studs. On that occasion it had seemed to work, and had been tried periodically since then. Now the Black Death convinced increasing numbers of people that desperate remedies were necessary. A letter, supposed to have fallen down from heaven, declaring that only Flagellants would be saved, was first published around 1260, but reappeared in 1343 in the Holy Land — it was supposed to have been delivered by an angel to the Church of St Peter in Jerusalem. Now waves of flagellation swept across Europe with all the hysteria of religious revivals. The Flagellants — mostly fairly respectable "pilgrims" of both sexes — would arrive in a town and hold their ceremony in the main square: they would strip to the waist, then flog themselves into an increasing state of hysteria until blood ran down to their feet, staining the white linen which was the traditional dress on the lower half of the body. The pilgrimage would last for thirty-three days, and each flagellant would have taken a vow to flog himself, or herself, three times a day for the whole of that time. A Master also moved among them, thrashing those who had failed in their vows.

As Flagellants themselves carried the plague from city to city, public opinion suddenly turned against them. The magistrates of Erfurt refused them entry, and no one objected. It was best not to wait until the Flagellants were within a town to raise objections, for their own frenzy made them violent, and they were likely to attack the objectors — one Dominican friar in Tournai was stoned to death. Human beings seem to be glad of an excuse to change their opinions, and only a year after they had been generally regarded with respect and admiration, the Flagellants were suddenly attacked as outcasts and cranks. The Pope issued a bull against them, and the hysteria vanished as abruptly as it had begun.

One of the major effects of the Black Death was a shortage of manpower; hundreds of villages became deserted because there were no men left to work the land. But the wealthy landlords themselves were forced to sell land to the peasants because it had become useless to them. And this meant a change in the balance of power. For centuries, the peasants had regarded themselves as little more than slaves. Suddenly, the Middle Ages were at an end. Suddenly, the peasants could pick and choose. In England in 1381, they rose up in revolt when King Richard the Second tried to impose a Poll Tax, and the king only succeeded in saving himself by promising them everything they wanted, then betraying them.

But nothing could put back the clock. For more than a thousand years, all the power in the world had been divided between the king and the Church. Now the ordinary people wanted their share. A "mad priest of Kent" called John Ball preached a doctrine that we would now call Communism — that all property should be held in common, and that there should be no more serfs or lords. He was executed immediately after the Peasants' Revolt; but his ideas

Luther burning the Papal Bull, 1520.

continued to spread. A reformer called John Wycliffe caused deep offense by declaring that Christ is man's only overlord, and that priests should not own property. Fortunately, he lived in England, and the Pope could not get at him, since England was at war with France, and regarded the Pope as no better than a Frenchman.

A Bohemian preacher called John Huss was less lucky. In 1415, the Church lured him to a "debate" with a promise of safe conduct, then seized him and burned him alive. It was a piece of treachery that would cost the Church very dear indeed. For now nothing could stop the spread of rebellion. And when a young German monk named Martin Luther went to Rome in 1510 and was disgusted by the commercialism of the Church, the days of the Pope's absolute authority were numbered.

The Great Protest

On 31 October, 1517 – All Saints Day – Martin Luther nailed a placard to the door of the Castle church in Wittenberg, criticizing the Roman Catholic Church in ninety five paragraphs. He objected that Rome had become rich, self-indulgent and corrupt. When Pope Leo the Tenth heard about it, he remarked: "Luther is just a drunken German – he will feel different when he is sober."

His casual dismissal proved to be a mistake. Within three years, Luther was the most famous man in Germany, and the revolution against the Church had started. If he had been an Italian or a Frenchman he would have been seized and burned. But the German princes resented collecting money for the Pope, and were glad of an excuse to stop doing it. Monks and nuns left their monasteries and married. Priests began to recite the mass in German. Reformers began smashing sacred statues in churches. And the poor and oppressed peasants began to revolt on a massive scale – the greatest scale so far in history. But at the height of his notoriety, Luther had to spend six months in hiding in the Wartburg castle – otherwise, he would certainly have gone to the stake like so many other reformers.

Muntzer the Messiah

In 1520, the year the Pope excommunicated Luther, one of Luther's most ardent young followers was already preparing to go further than the master. His name was Thomas Muntzer, and he had spent years studying the Fathers of the Church and reading their works in Greek and Hebrew. Now, in the town of Zwickau, he came under the influence of a strange messiah named Niklas Storch. Storch was a self-taught weaver who was convinced that the end of the world was at hand. First the Turks would conquer the world, then the Antichrist would rule over it, then God's Elect would rise up and defeat the wicked in battle. When that happened, the Last Judgement would begin.

When he met Storch, Thomas Muntzer was already growing dissatisfied with the teachings of Luther. Luther taught that man does not need the Church to forgive his sins; he only needs faith in God. Muntzer went a step further. Man can actually *communicate* with God and hear his voice. Once this happens, a man becomes the vessel of the holy spirit, and he actually *becomes God*.

Muntzer, who had been a bookish young man, now suddenly abandoned reading, and went preaching among the poor, particularly the silver miners and the weavers of Zwickau. He said such unpleasant things about the Catholics in the area, and even about Luther, that the Town Council dismissed him. His friend Storch led an uprising, which had to be suppressed by force. Many weavers were arrested. Muntzer went off to Prague — which, a century later, was still seething with anger about the execution of John Huss — and told his audiences that he was founding a new church which would consist solely of the Elect. The Town Council lost no time in expelling him.

He became a wandering preacher for the next two years, suffering great hardship — which only deepened his sense of mission. In 1523 he was invited to become curate in the small Thuringian town of Allstedt, where he performed the Latin service in German, and became a celebrated preacher. Peasants came from miles around to hear him. But so did

Duke John of Saxony, who was worried about what he heard of this revolutionary firebrand. At his request, Muntzer preached a sermon stating his belief that the Millennium was at hand, and would be preceded by great battles and appalling suffering. Duke John went away looking deeply thoughtful, and Muntzer congratulated himself on impressing him.

Perhaps he did. But when some of his followers came to Allstedt, telling him that they had been evicted from their homes by their landlords, he began to change his opinion of Duke John, and preached a sermon declaring that tyrants were about to be overthrown and the Millennium about to begin. Martin Luther heard about Muntzer's Messianic ideas, and wrote an open letter to the Princes of Saxony warning them about Muntzer. Muntzer replied with a pamphlet accusing Luther of being (with some confusion of the sexes) the Whore of Babylon, and a corrupt slave of the ruling classes.

This was hardly fair to Duke John and his elder brother Frederick the Wise, who were amongst the most tolerant princes of the time. Luther had raised tremendous political storms, most of which centred in their territories, and they were doing their best to remain open-minded. So they sent for Muntzer and asked him what the devil he thought he was up to. The hearing at which he was asked to defend himself lasted several days. In all probability, he would have been sent back to Allstedt with a warning to behave himself. But Muntzer decided not to wait for the result. He climbed over the Weimar city wall one night and made his way to the city of Mulhausen, which was in the midst of a power struggle between the poor — led by another revolutionary called Heinrich Pfeiffer — and the respectable burghers. The burghers soon ejected him. But a few months later, Pfeiffer took power from the Town Council, and Muntzer hurried back.

By the time he arrived, Germany had plunged into its own Peasants' Revolt. The poor were on the march, inspired by Luther (who hastened to disown them), and they skirmished with the troops of the local princes, and attacked monasteries and nunneries.

By May 1525, Muntzer was heading his own peasant army of about eight thousand, and was determined to lead them to the victory foretold in the scriptures. There can be no doubt that he was now convinced that he was a Messiah — or at least, a reincarnation of the prophet Daniel. His chosen symbols were the sword and the rainbow.

His luck took a turn for the worse when Frederick the Wise died, and was succeeded by Duke John. The Duke finally decided that he had to take sides. He appealed to the young commander Philip of Hesse, who had just put down a rising in his own territories, to come and do the same in Thuringia.

Muntzer summoned his own forces and marched out to meet him. The two armies faced one another on 15 May, 1525, Philip's highly trained and well equipped army looking down on the unruly mob of peasants — armed with clubs and pick axes — from a hilltop. Philip experienced a softening of the heart. He sent a message offering not to attack if the peasants would hand over Muntzer. The peasants looked up at the army looming above them, and suddenly felt that this was not such a bad idea. But Muntzer once more revealed his skill as a leader; he made a magnificent speech in which he promised them victory and immunity from the cannons. "I will catch their cannonballs in my sleeves!"

As he spoke, a rainbow appeared in the sky. His followers needed no further convincing, and marched to confront the enemy. As they came closer, Philip of Hesse ordered his cannons to open fire. As the balls cut a swathe through their ranks, the peasants turned and scattered in panic. Philip's cavalry cut them down as they fled. It was a total rout, and six thousand peasants were to die.

Thomas Muntzer escaped to nearby Frankenhausen, but the triumphant army soon overran the town. Soon afterwards, they took Mulhausen too. Muntzer was found hiding in a cellar in Frankenhausen, and was taken captive

Anabaptists taking the Sacrament.

and tortured. On 27 May, 1425, he and Heinrich Pfeiffer were beheaded. That was virtually the end of Germany's Peasants' Revolt.

The surviving peasants felt nothing but bitterness against Luther. But in retrospect it seems clear that Luther did the right thing. If he had supported the revolt, he would have been executed like Muntzer, and Protestantism would have died. As it was, a law was passed declaring that each German state could make up its own mind whether it wanted to be Protestant or Catholic. The majority opted for Lutheranism. Luther married a nun who had escaped from a convent, had six children, and died at the age of sixty-three, nearly thirty years after he had started the revolution with his ninety five theses.

The Massacre of the Anabaptists

The most horrifying episode of this bloody religious war was still to come — the slaughter of the Anabaptists of Munster, under their leader John of Leyden.

Although the German princes had won the Peasants' War, the spirit of Thomas Muntzer marched on. In these times of revolt and misery — a new outbreak of the Black Death killed thousands more in 1529 — the poor continued to believe that the Day of Judgement *must* be at hand. The followers of Muntzer called themselves Anabaptists (or re-baptizers — they believed that Christians have to be re-baptized in adulthood), and after Muntzer's death, his torch was taken up by a visionary called Melchior Hoffmann, who also taught that the end of the world was at hand. Unlike Muntzer, Hoffmann was a peaceable man who advised his followers to wait quietly for the Millennium. But this did not save him. When he proclaimed that Strasbourg was the New Jerusalem in 1533, and that the Last Trumpet was about to sound, his followers held their breath, and so did the burghers of Strasbourg. But when the year passed without any sign of the end of the world, Hoffmann was seized by the Town Council of Strasbourg and hung up in a cage to die slowly.

In Munster, the capital of Westphalia, a new Anabaptist prophet called Bernard Rothmann preached against Catholicism; his future father-in-law, a rich businessman called Bernard Knipperdolling, gave him full support. The two fanatics ran through the streets calling on the populace to repent, and dozens of nuns who had deserted their nunneries joined in the hysteria, and began writhing on the ground and having visions. Munster was beginning to look like a madhouse, and as Anabaptists from a neighbouring duchy flooded in, the Prince-Bishop of Munster, Francis von Waldeck, began to feel deeply uneasy. And when disciples of a prophet called Jan Matthyson arrived and

89

Cults and Fanatics

announced that Munster was the New Jerusalem, even the Protestants began to move out. One of the leading disciples was a tall, handsome, bearded man called Jan Bockelson, who, because he came from Leyden, was known as John of Leyden.

Soon the messiah Jan Matthyson arrived, accompanied by his beautiful wife, an ex-nun. He proved to be as tall and handsome as John of Leyden, and when he stood up in the market place, dressed in flowing robes and carrying two tablets under his arms, and told the populace that their city had been chosen by God to be the New Jerusalem, they applauded wildly. Soon the whole town was awash with religious ecstasy – the women playing a leading role. People had visions every day, and – in the manner of the Brethren of the Free Spirit – felt that all this direct contact with God entitled them to a little sexual license – after all, what was the point of being involved in a great religious upheaval if you had to stay chaste?

A nineteenth century depiction of a group of Anabaptists.

In February 1534, the worst fears of the Catholics were realized when the Anabaptists were overwhelmingly elected to the Town Council and became, in effect, the rulers of the city. Catholic churches and homes were sacked. Catholics who refused to be converted were driven naked out of the city. The weather was freezing, and many died.

Munster was surrounded by Bishop von Waldeck's soldiers, but the Anabaptists were not afraid. God was on their side. And at Easter, the prophet Matthyson had a vision that convinced him that he could raise the seige with a few followers. The next day he issued forth with twenty men – and was promplty cut down. The soldiers displayed his head on a pike where it could be seen from the city walls.

Now John of Leyden was the leader. A bankrupt tailor to whom life had not been kind, he had become the main hope of thousands of enthusiasts. The city of Munster now became a religious commonwealth in the most literal sense – that is, John of Leyden preached the common ownership of property, and made the citizens take their meals all together in great dining halls. He also had an idea that made him even more popular. Men and women were sexually free. A man could take as many wives as he wanted, and a woman who wanted to become somebody's wife merely had to go and join his household. There was an understandable rush to get into the Prophet's bed, and John of Leyden soon found himself trying to satisfy sixteen women.

Life in the New Jerusalem was delightful; the summer of 1534 turned into one long party, in which the citizens ate their way though twelve hundred oxen and vast quantities of cheese and fish. There were endless processions and banquets. Traitors and unbelievers were executed to provide the populace with entertainment. Money was abolished, but medallions were struck showing John of Leyden's face surrounded by the legend "The Word Made Flesh".

Meanwhile, the bishop was beginning to despair of ever taking the town; the enthusiatic soldiers of the prophet –

1,700 of them – repelled every attack. But as winter drew on, other princes sent reinforcements. Now the Anabaptists were in real trouble, and discovered that it had been a mistake to eat their food in such quantity as they were driven to eat cats, dogs and rats. At Easter, exactly a year after the death of Jan Matthyson, the beseiging general demanded the surrender of the city. After months of starvation, hundreds had died and the rest were living skeletons. Yet still John of Leyden's faith and oratory sustained them. God was merely testing them; victory would soon be theirs. When Bernard Knipperdolling's mistress tried to escape from the city, he killed her with his own hands.

After more weeks of starvation, John of Leyden declared generously that any who wished to leave the city could do so. Parents with children felt this was their last chance, and about nine hundred marched out through the gates. But they were worse off than ever, for the armies refused to let them pass, and they were forced to starve to death outside the walls.

In June, four of John's followers decided they had had enough; the whole town stank of rotting flesh. They slipped out of Munster, and told the enemy general how some of his men could enter the city unobserved. On Midsummer's Eve, 24 June, 1535, four hundred soldiers entered the city quietly after dark. When they were discovered the next morning, fierce fighting broke out; it looked as if the intruders were about to be massacred. But the bishop's forces chose this moment to make another attack on the walls, selecting the weak spots that the traitors had pointed out. The fighting lasted all day, but the inhabitants were weak with hunger, and on 25 June, Leyden fell. John of Leyden, Bernard Knipperdolling, and a leader named Krechting, were dragged before the Bishop and humiliated. Three hundred Anabaptists were promised a safe conduct if they surrendered, then were massacred. The two "queens" of John of Leyden and Knipperdolling were beheaded. (Bernard Rothmann disappeared, perhaps killed in the fighting and mutilated beyond recognition.)

The Bishop could not resist engaging John of Leyden in debate, but the ex-messiah proved more than a match for him. When the Bishop said he received his authority from the Pope, John replied that he had received his from God and His Prophets.

For the next six months, the three Anabaptists were dragged in chains around the neighbouring towns and publicly exhibited. In January 1536, they were horribly put to death in the main square of Leyden. Chained to a stake, John of Leyden had his flesh torn off with red hot pincers; incredibly, he did not cry out. But the pain was finally too much and he begged for mercy. The Bishop smiled grimly and ordered that his tongue should be torn out. Then his heart was pierced with a red hot dagger.

Knipperdolling had tried to beat out his brains against a wall, then to strangle himself, but the executioner was too strong for him. He and Krechting were tortured to death as slowly as John of Leyden, while the Bishop watched from a window opposite. Then the torn and burnt bodies were hung in cages from the tower of St Lambert Church, where Bernard Rothmann had originally declared the coming of the Millennium.

The death of John of Leyden served much the same purpose as the death of Simon bar Kochba or Sabbatai Zevi; it punctured the pretensions of messiahs for a long time to come. Some Anabaptists came to England, and because many of them lived in communes, they became known as Familists. Their founder was a Munster Anabaptist named Henry Nicholas, known as H.N. (which also stood for *homo novus* – New Man), and his group had become known as the Family of Love. They declared that the essence of religion was simply love, and that no other law was needed. In 1575 they petitioned the British parliament for toleration, but five years later, Queen Elizabeth declared that they should be put down as a "damnable sect".

Cults and Fanatics

Eleven years later, a man called Hacket, who had proclaimed himself the Supreme Lord of the World, was executed for treason, threatening God to rend his throne in two if He did not save him. God declined to intervene.

In the reign of Charles I, a curious sect known as Ranters preached many of the same doctrines as the Brethren of the Free Spirit: that sin was an illusion, and that therefore adultery, drunkenness, swearing and even theft were not crimes at all. In 1650, Cromwell tried to suppress them with a Blasphemy Act, but was only partly successful. On the other hand, a remarkable prophet named George Fox, who was wandering around England at the same time, and attacking organized religion as contemptuously as any messiah in history, succeeded in impressing Oliver Cromwell, and went on to become the founder of the Quakers, or Society of Friends. (The word "quaker" was applied contemptuously, meaning that they quaked with fear as they talked about the Wrath to Come.)

His friend and disciple James Naylor was less lucky. Female disciples convinced him that he was the Messiah, and he allowed them to persuade him to ride into Bristol as Christ had ridden into Jerusalem. Women shouted "Holy, holy, holy is the Lord God of Israel", and threw down their cloaks before his horse's hoofs. He was promptly arrested. Tried in November 1656, he admitted to the judges that he was the Son of God as well as a prophet, and his female disciples assured the judges that this was so. He was sentenced to have his tongue burnt through, and to be branded on the forehead with a letter B for Blasphemer. After that, he was whipped and imprisoned in a damp cell for three years.

It ruined his health, and he died in 1660, soon after his release, when setting out on a preaching expedition. And so another promising messiah experienced the downfall that seems inevitable for prophets who succumb to delusions of grandeur.

94

Chapter Five

Messiahs in the Land of Opportunity

A fter the cruelty and bloodshed of the past two chapters, it is a relief to emerge into the calmer waters of the nineteenth century, when a messiah was no longer in danger of being tortured or burnt at the stake. We are in a new atmosphere of tolerance – and of gullibility: an observation that is perfectly illustrated by the amazing case of Saint Matthias.

The Poisonous Prophet

M athews discovered the power of belief early in life. In 1797, when he was nine-years-old, he decided that the fruit and sweets being shared around his class at school rightfully belonged to him. He told the other children that his uncle, the "Man of the Thunder", lived in a passing storm cloud and that he would be angry if the sweets were not all given to his nephew. A moment later, thunder rumbled across the sky and Robert received an armful of goodies from his frightened classmates.

What to most children might only have been an amusing confidence trick had a deeper impact on Robert Mathews. He developed an increasing conviction that he was one of the "chosen". As part of his training for his mission he decided to become a carpenter's apprentice when he was sixteen on the grounds that it was a "divine trade".

Cults and Fanatics

After his apprenticeship he wandered the state, plying his trade and teaching his interpretation of the gospel. His frenetic preaching style earned him the nickname "Jumpin' Jesus" and he would often stand up in church and dispute with the preacher. He married and settled down in Albany, New York State.

After several years of relatively quiet home living, Mathews suddenly decided that he must take his children "out into the wilderness", and set-off for the deep woods before his distraught wife could stop him. Fortunately, he and his half-starved children were found by a search-party of concerned neighbours a few days later. Mathews was apparently relieved to have the children taken to safety, but insisted on staying in the woods himself. It was here, a few days later, that he received the divine revelation that he was in fact the reincarnation of Saint Matthew and was thenceforth to preach the new message — as revealed to him personally by God — as the Prophet Matthias.

At about this time a similar revelation occurred to Elijah Pierson, a rich and successful New York businessman, although in a considerably less biblical setting. He was sitting on an omnibus travelling down Wall Street, when an angel appeared to him alone and proclaimed that he was the reincarnation of the Prophet Elijah and henceforth he must be about the Lord's work.

Pierson immediately set about organizing a Holy Club, recruiting members from many who had become disillusioned with orthodox Christianity. He also set up a mission in the Bowery Hill red light district to bring the prostitutes to the Lord because, he said, they were "the descendants of Mary Magdalen".

When his wife became seriously ill Pierson assured her and his flock that, should she pass on, she would be resurrected to help continue their work. She died as her husband sat praying over her fervently and anointing her with oils. When this failed to revive her, Pierson announced that he had seen a vision of the Prophet of the Lord whose coming would set all to rights. He instructed his flock and even his household staff to be in readiness for the great event.

Meanwhile, the Prophet Matthias was establishing himself. Having grown a suitably bushy beard and changed his preaching style from the frenetic to the portentous, he travelled to New York in search of a rich benefactor. Proclaiming his message of vegetarianism, temperance and faith in the word of the Lord, he made a convert of a wealthy businessman called Mills.

Convinced that Matthias was a genuine prophet, Mills virtually begged him to accept money. Saint Matthias was robed in finest purple silk with trappings to match. Mills was also ordered to commission a set of plates mounted with the lion of the tribe of Judah and two silver chalices for the Prophet's exclusive use.

Unfortunately for Saint Matthias, Mills' family were less than enthusiastic about the turn of events; they had Mills packed-off to the Bloomingdale Lunatic Asylum. When Matthias threatened them with Hell and Damnation they arranged to have him committed to the Department of the Insane Poor at Bellevue Hospital. After an ignominious period behind bars he was released. But he had enjoyed his period of affluence so much that he determined that this was how he intended to live in the future. He now went to call on a friend of Mr Mills, one Elijah Pierson.

When he arrived at Pierson's house the door was answered by the black cook, Isabella, who was a Holy Club convert. She asked him timorously; "Art thou the Lord?"

"I am," he boomed without hesitation and strode in.

Pierson spoke to the stranger for several hours, by the end of which time he was convinced Matthias was he who was foretold. The Prophet rewarded his faith by proclaiming that Pierson was not only the reincarnation of the

Prophet Elijah, but also of John the Baptist. Matthias then settled into his new patrons home and proceeded to live like a king.

The next convert was a well-off friend of Pierson's, Benjamin Folger. Folger was at first alarmed about the holy man and warned his friend of "the workings of false prophets", but Matthias' combination of bombast and biblical quotation soon won him over. As one of his first contributions to the new spiritual kingdom, Folger purchased Matthias a jewel-encrusted sword with which to "smite the devil" and yet more purple robes, this time trimmed with silver and gold.

In fact, the Prophet's spiritual kingdom seemed to demand large amounts of material wealth. In September, 1822, he was taken for a trip to Mr and Mrs Folger's summer home at Sing Sing. He liked it very much and informed them that he had received a vision to the effect that Folger was to give the house to the servant of the Lord. His disciple faithfully complied, as did Elijah Pierson when the Prophet demanded the deeds to his luxurious house on Third Street, New York, together with its contents.

It was not long before all of Pierson's and Folger's property had been placed at the Prophet's disposal, as well as tens of thousands of dollars. Thus fortified against the works of the devil, Saint Matthias decided that he and his flock of elect should all move to Mount Zion – his name for Folger's summer home in Sing Sing. The elect consisted of Pierson and his daughter Elizabeth, the Folgers and their children and Isabella, the devout black cook who had first recognized the Prophet of the Lord.

Unfortunately, there was little peace at Mount Zion. Comfort inspired Saint Matthias to behave like a tyrant. Lying at ease all day, served like a sultan, he would only assume the vertical position to berate his disciples. Any sign of backsliding or hint of dissent would unleash a torrent of abuse and recrimination. Indeed, his Hell and Damnation sermons often lasted so long that one started at breakfast would leave his followers no time to wash the dishes for lunch.

He also devised some unusual ceremonies — for example, he would bathe in a tub of water, then call his naked disciples to gather about him so that he could sprinkle them with the water he had thus purified.

At some point he decided that Mrs Folger was his soulmate and the "Mother of the Kingdom", explaining to her husband that she should be relinquished to him. As Folger wavered, his wife suddenly announced that she had seen a vision that confirmed that she was the Prophet's wife and a virgin in the sight of Heaven; under such divine pressure the unhappy Folger felt obliged to agree. As a consolation prize, Matthias offered him his own daughter, then living with her mother and husband in Albany. Oddly enough the Prophet's son-in-law agreed to the arrangement — at least, after Folger had bribed him with a gold watch.

Soon the goings-on began to deeply worry Elijah/St John Pierson. Being forced to do menial work was not how he saw the role of a double prophet, and he began to experience the sin of doubt. After violent arguments with the Prophet he left Mount Zion, taking his daughter and the deeds to his house in Westchester County. But his respite was only temporary. Within a week Saint Matthias and his entourage had come to visit.

In what seemed a peace gesture, Matthias went out to pick a big bowl of blackberries, a favourite dessert of Pierson's. Two others tried a few at dinner, but said they tasted bitter and left them. Pierson, however, ate a good many and became very sick. He vomited continuously, suffered epileptic fits and became partially paralysed. The Prophet stood over the suffering man and declared that he had encouraged fifty devils to enter himself by his sin of dissent and those who tried to help him would suffer a similar fate. No doctor was sent for.

After two days Pierson seemed to recover enough to shuffle about the house, but the Prophet threatened damnation to any who communicated with the sick man. On the fifth day of his illness, Pierson was found lying on his bedroom floor in a coma. The Prophet ordered that he be placed on a pallet of straw and poured cold water over him to wake him from his "hellish sleep". Not surprisingly, Pierson never regained consciousness and died eight days after he had eaten the blackberries. The Prophet then acknowledged that he had indeed killed Pierson – by making a certain holy sign over him, a gesture that invariably led to the death of his enemies.

Despite such alarming manifestations of his power, the kingdom of Saint Matthias was falling apart. His soulmate (the ex-Mrs Folger) seemed to lose faith in him when she gave birth to their child – prophesied to be a son who would be heir to the kingdom – and it turned out to be a girl. Her ex-husband also seemed to experience doubt when he discovered that the Prophet had bankrupted him. Both asked Saint Matthias to leave their house. He complied reluctantly, but within a week he was back, threatening that sickness would follow if they turned from the light. They insisted and he left again. That same morning, the entire Folger family became sick with violent stomach cramps and continuous vomiting. Fortunately, they all recovered.

This time Matthias had gone too far. He was arrested and charged with murder and in April, 1835, his trial began. The Prophet, on entering the court, made his usual dramatic impression by declaring that those who dared sit in judgment on him were "Damned! Damned! DAMNED!" When the judge restored order he added contempt of court to the charge sheet.

Twelve years later, the Prophet would almost certainly have been found guilty of murder and attempted murder; both Pierson and the Folgers had showed every sign of arsenic poisoning. Indeed, Pierson's exhumed body should have provided more than enough evidence to send Matthias to the gallows. But the Marsh test for arsenic was not invented until 1847 and American doctors seemed unfamiliar with other European tests. Eventually the case dismissed for lack of evidence. The Prophet served only four months in jail for his contempt of court, and for assaulting his daughter (he had beaten her with a leather belt for being impiously rude to Mrs Folger).

After serving his sentence he went west, still proclaiming his sainthood, but his reputation preceded him. Newspaper revelations about life at Mount Zion had shocked and titillated readers throughout the United States, and his claims to near-divinity no longer convinced. Fortunately, he was no longer in need of money. He had taken eighty thousand dollars from Pierson alone, of which the daughter Elizabeth was able to recoup only seven thousand dollars through legal action.

In his later years he met Joseph Smith, the founder of the Mormon Church of the Latter Day Saints, and they talked all night. Smith later described him as "a brilliant intellect but a mind full of darkness".

Smith himself was one of the rare — and unfortunate — prophets who arouse his fellow countrymen to murderous rage; his story forms an interesting contrast to that of the egregious Saint Matthew.

The Mormons

Smith, born in 1805, was the son of a Vermont farmer, and when he was ten, his father, Joseph senior moved to Palmyra, New York, with his wife and nine children. It was a period of feverish religious activity in America, with various sects — Methodist, Presbyterian, Baptist — expanding at an explosive rate as they made new converts.

Dr Cyrus Teed, known to his followers as Koresh, believed that the earth was hollow, and that life existed only upon the internal surface. He had been led to this conclusion by a personal conviction that the universe could not be infinite. If it was not, then, surely it must have form and boundaries? The boundary, Teed concluded, was the earth beneath our feet. Everything above our heads was contained within the earth, with the sun being the cosmic centre.

Dr Teed travelled America during the 1870s, spreading his message and accumulating devotees. In 1888 The Koreshan Unity was formed in Chicago, a community of "cellularists" who also believed in earth-power and the possibility of immortality and resurrection. Like the Flat Earthers, the Koreshan community carried out scientific experiments on a straight section of canal, eventually concluding that the earth's apparent convexity was caused by optical illusion. Fired by a need to experiment further, "Koresh" moved his following to Estero in Florida, where a flat coastline provided an ideal testing ground. There, a carefully made series of wooden frames were extended across the water, beginning at 128 inches above sea level and carrying on for 4¼18 miles. If the experiment was carried out on the outside of a globe, the distance between the end of the line and the water should increase; Teed found that it decreased, proving to his satisfaction that he was standing inside the earth.

The Koreshan community, despite antagonizing Florida locals by block voting for their own candidates, thrived. In 1908, three days before Christmas, Dr Teed died. The Koreshans were expecting him to rise on Christmas Day, but when he did not, they were ordered by the authorities to get his body in the ground before it became unhygienic. A large tomb was built on Estero Island and Koresh deposited within. A few years later the entire tomb was washed away, leaving no trace. The Koreshans continue to live in Florida, having built a college to continue their ideas.

Joseph's mother Lucy became a convert to Presbyterianism, which had been established by John Calvin in Geneva in 1536, as did two of Joseph's brothers and his sister Sophronia. Joseph attended meetings of the various warring sects, and as he listened to them denouncing one another, he gave a great deal of thought to religion.

In the spring of 1820, after reading a passage in the *Epistle of James* which declared that those in perplexity should ask God, he went into a grove of trees to pray. There he had a revelation — a pillar of light descended, in which he saw two men; one of these pointed to the other and said: "This is my beloved son. Hear him!". Smith then asked God which sect he ought to join, and was told: "None of them." They were all wrong, and all creeds were an abomination in His sight. When Joseph came to his senses he was lying on his back. Back at home he told his mother that he had just learned that Presbyterianism was not true.

The revelation had no profound effect on him, and he later admitted that he continued to enjoy "jovial company" and to behave in a way that was not suitable for one who had been "called of God".

Three and a half years later, on 21 September, 1823, Joseph was saying his prayers in bed when the light appeared again, and he saw a man dressed in a white robe "whose feet did not touch the floor". The visitor explained that he was an angel called Moroni, who went on to talk at length about the scriptures, then told Joseph that he had written a history of the ancient inhabitants of America on plates of gold. After this, Moroni ascended to heaven in a shaft of light. A few minutes later he reappeared, and repeated everything he had just said, then vanished as before. Soon he was back again, repeating it yet again. The next day, he reappeared as Joseph (in a state of understandable fatigue) was crossing a field, and described where the plates were to be found.

Obeying his instructions, Joseph went to a hill called Cumorah, about four miles away. On the top, he found a large stone, which he levered up with a pole. In the hole underneath was a box, and in this he found some gold plates, a breastplate, and a pair of silver spectacles – which Moroni had called Urim and Thummim – and which would enable him to translate the words on the gold plates.

Smith was not allowed to take them yet. The angel showed him a vision of the heavens, and also of the Prince of Darkness and his legions, then explained that Joseph must spend four years of preparation in order to become worthy of translating the plates.

In 1827, Smith was finally allowed to take the gold plates away with him. He carried them home in a borrowed buggy, but seems to have showed them to no one, not even his wife Emma, who went with him to collect them. Two months later, with fifty dollars presented by his first disciple, a farmer called Martin Harris, Smith and his wife went to Harmony, Pennsylvania, and there Joseph settled down to translating the plates with the aid of the silver spectacles. He did this behind a screen, so that no one actually saw the

A Mormon gathering in Salt Lake City.

plates. Martin Harris called at some point, and took away a piece of paper with a transcription of some of the characters on it — they were apparently in a script called "reformed Egyptian" — and showed them to a New York professor named Anton, who gave him a certificate saying that the characters were genuine. But when he heard that they had been obtained from an angel, Anton tore up his certificate.

So the *Book of Mormon* came into existence. It told how America had been originally settled by people from the Tower of Babel in the fifth century AD. These settlers gradually degenerated into men of violence. Eleven hundred years later, more settlers arrived in Chile, including four brothers. From one of the brothers, who was fair, descended a white race, the Nephites; from the other three, who were dark, descended the Indians (or Lamonites). After his death on the cross, Jesus Christ appeard in America and preached the gospel. And in AD 385, after the Nephites

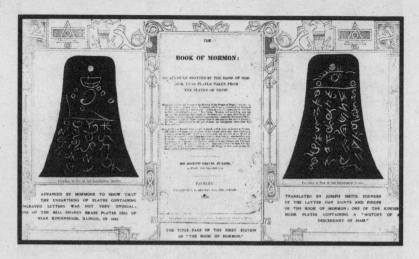

The book of Mormon.

were almost wiped out by the Lamanites near the Hill Cumorah, their prophet Mormon wrote the history, which was then buried in the hill.

Martin Harris mortgaged his farm to provide the cash for publication, and *The Book of Mormon* appeared in 1830. Meanwhile, the gold plates had been returned to the Angel Moroni, no one but Smith having even glimpsed them, although a young schoolteacher named Oliver Cowdery helped with the translation from the other side of the screen. The first 116 pages of the manuscript had already been lost when Martin Harris's indignant wife threw them on the fire.

Reviews of the book were contemptuous; no one had any doubt that Smith was a confidence trickster who had invented the whole story. But the critiques at least aroused curiosity, and Smith soon began to accumulate followers. He also began to accumulate enemies, and decided to move to some less hostile state. The Latter Day Saints – as the Mormons now called themselves – decided to move west. The "missionaries" had already established a church in Kirtland, Ohio. There Smith received a revelation that declared that all members of the Church should deed their property to the community, and a bishop would give each family back what he felt they required. As with John of Leyden, it was a kind of communism in practice.

Problems arose. The citizens of Kirtland objected to the Saints as the citizens of Munster had objected to the Anabaptists. In 1836, the Saints established their own bank and printed their own money; in 1837, it collapsed, causing much hardship; five of Smith's twelve "apostles" denounced him as a fallen prophet, and left. Smith saw it all as a test of the faithful.

Other Saints had already established themselves in Missouri; Smith joined them there. By now even Martin Harris and Oliver Cowdery had left in disillusionment. When angry mobs drove the Mormons out of Missouri – after Smith had spent several months in jail – they moved on to found the town of Nauvoo in Illinois. But Illinois' inhabitants proved to be as hostile as those of Missouri. Smith may have made things worse in July 1843 by publishing a document declaring that God had ordained polygamy, or "plural marriage" – although at this stage it was not openly announced. (Smith himself must have been practising plural marriage long before he announced its legality, for he seems to have married at least twenty-seven women, and possibly as many as forty-eight.) Finally, a dispute with the governor became so bitter that, early in 1844, Smith decided it was time to go further west to found a City of the Saints.

Governor Ford was worried as the surrounding communities armed themselves and talked about massacring the Saints. In June, Smith and his associates – including his brother Hyrum – were charged with "riot". Convinced that he would be killed, he decided to flee, but then changed his mind and returned to give himself up. This seemed to defuse the threatened violence, and Joseph Smith, his brother Hyrum, and two followers, were lodged in Carthage jail.

On 27 June, 1844, at four in the afternoon, a hundred men rushed the jail. Governor Ford had marched his forces off to Nauvoo to restore order, and there were only eight men in charge of the prisoners. Hyrum was shot by a bullet that came through the window, and collapsed on the floor. Joseph Smith opened the door and emptied his six shooter into the mob. Then the attackers flung open the door and began shooting. One of the disciples, John Taylor, tried to jump out of the window, but was hit by a bullet. Joseph Smith attempted to leave the same way, and was hit several times; he fell out of the window, twenty feet from the ground. Staring out of the window after him, the other disciple, Willard Richards, saw that he seemed to be dead.

A cry of "The Mormons are coming" caused the crowd to scatter, and Taylor and Richards managed to take refuge in a safer part of the jail. In fact, no Mormons were coming. But since Joseph Smith and his brother were now dead, the crowd dispersed.

It was left to Smith's chief lieutenant, Brigham Young, to lead the Saints on their great trek westward, to the place where, in 1847, they founded Salt Lake City. With tremendous energy they irrigated the desert, and arranged the transportation of thousands of converts from Europe. (The Mormons always attached great importance to proseltysing.) When Young announced the doctrine of polygamy in 1852, he was deprived of the governorship of the territory. "Plural marriage" was finally disowned by the Church in 1890, but when Young died in 1877 he had seventeen wives and fifty-six children.

Mormonism – as can be seen – always aroused fierce opposition. As early as 1834, E.D. Howe, an investigative journalist of the period, published a collection of affidavits from friends and neighbours of Smith who described him as a lazy and mendacious religious con man. Another investigator discovered a novel by the Reverend Simon Spalding that was alleged to be the true source of the *Book of Mormon*. In the mid-1920s, Brigham H. Roberts, the official historian of the Mormon Church, appealed to Church leaders to "help him resolve problems" about the *Book of Mormon*, one of which was that it contained so many similarities to a book called *A View of the Hebrews* published in 1823 by the Reverend Ethan Smith. Another problem was that the *Book of Mormon* refers to the ancient Hebrews use of steel, and to domestic animals that were unknown in ancient times. Referring to many similar discrepancies, Roberts concluded: "The evidence, I sorrowfully submit, points to Joseph Smith as their creator." Whether or not this is true, Smith remains one of the most charismatic and influential messiahs of the nineteenth century.

The Oneida Community

Smith's advocacy of plural marriage was undoubtedly one of the chief causes of later hostility to the Mormons. Another prophet from Vermont whose views caused equal indignation nevertheless succeeded in avoiding martyrdom, and established one of the most successful and prosperous communities in the history of religious dissent.

To his disciples, John Humphrey Noyes was an inspired prophet and a great spiritual leader, but to most of his contemporaries he was a libertine whose doctrines of free love and "complex marriage" were a danger to the community. There were many strange religious communities in America in the nineteenth century: the Shakers (so called because they went into convulsions of religious ecstasy that made them shake all over), the Ephrata, the Rappites,

The Oneida community.

Zoarites and many others. Most of these were "Perfectionists" — that is, they rejected the notion that man is a miserable sinner as unnecessarily pessimistic and taught that, through Divine Grace, man can achieve perfection. The Shakers believed that God is both male and female by nature, so women were as important as men in their religious rites, many of which looked like orgies. But the Shakers taught the importance of strict chastity.

The 1830s and 1840s were a time of tremendous religious revivals in America, to such an extent that one portion of New York State was known as the Burnt Over Region because the fires of revivalism had burned so fiercely there. Men like Hiram Sheldon, Erasmus Stone and Jarvis Rider preached their gospel in the cotton village of Manlius and their converts adopted the name of the Saints. One of the subjects that fascinated them was whether the old marriage vows would still be binding when the New Heaven and New Earth arrived. (Most of the great religious revivals were based on the conviction that the Day of Judgment was just around the corner.) It was John Humphrey Noyes who provided a startling and controversial answer to that question.

John Humphrey Noyes was born at Brattleboro, Vermont, the son of a Congressman; he studied law, then divinity. He was a man of considerable magnetism and remarkable intellect and he seems to have spent the two years following his conversion (at the age of twenty) in religious broodings and wrestlings. He found that he simply could not accept that he was a miserable sinner. Then, when he was twenty-two, the answer suddenly revealed itself to him in a blinding flash of revelation. Reading the Gospel of St John, he could see clearly that Jesus had announced the Second Coming within one generation of his own lifetime — that is, in the year AD 70. But if Jesus had already come to earth, then the Kingdom of God was already here. In that case, why was there so much sin on earth? The answer must be because people were unaware of the Second Coming. This, Noyes could now see and explained why he himself could never feel that he was a sinner. He wasn't. He was already saved. All he had to do was to live according to the gospels and nothing could go wrong.

The Bible said that in heaven there would be no marriage or giving in marriage. The Shakers also accepted this and for them it meant an obligation to celibacy. Noyes did not agree. Sex is obviously necessary to continue the race. What the Bible meant was obviously that all men were married to all women and vice versa. In *The Battle Axe*, the newspaper of the Perfectionists, he published in 1837 a letter in which he explained that "at the marriage supper of the Lamb . . . every dish is free to every guest". Sexual intercourse is one of the best things of life — men and women were intended to "reflect upon each other the love of God". Sexual shame was a consequence of the Fall, so all

111

the Saved should now abandon it. Men and women should have sex together just as they felt inclined, regarding it as a sacrament.

At the age of twenty-three, Noyes returned to his home in Putney, Vermont, and preached his views; he converted a number of his own family. He married the daughter of the State Governor and one of his disciples, J.L. Skinner, married his sister. In 1840, Noyes and a number of disciples founded the Putney Community, which consisted of seven houses and a store on five hundred acres of fertile land. They spent the afternoons in manual labour to support themselves and the rest of the time in debate, prayer, reading, and teaching various subjects, including Latin, Greek and Hebrew.

Meanwhile, Noyes continued to brood on the problems posed by his doctrines of "free love". In 1846, he saw the answer. The problem with sexual intercourse was that it often produced unwanted results in the form of children. Mrs Harriet Noyes had produced five babies in six years and four had been stillborn. The answer was simple. Men and women should have full sexual intercourse, with orgasm taking place in the vagina only when they wished to produce children. For the rest of the time, the man must teach himself continence – not abstention. He could place his penis in the vagina but he must exercise severe self-discipline not to have an emission. It was a method that would later become known as the *karezza*, a term invented by Dr Alice Bunker Stockham of Ohio. Noyes pointed out that this method "*vastly increases* pleasure" (his italics). This doctrine was complemented by the notion of "complex marriage" – that every man should regard all women as his wives and vice versa.

Noyes was not a man to keep his ideas secret – religious prophets seldom are – and he preached "male continence" (i.e. the *karezza*) and "complex marriage" quite openly. His neighbours were naturally outraged at what they took to be a public rejection of all decency. (Even nowadays, a community with these ideas would probably have a hard time of it if they lived in the vicinity of a small town.) There was public outrage and the following year, Noyes was indicted on a charge of adultery. He decided that his great vision was too important to be destroyed by a few bigots. Fortunately, some of his disciples had already set up a community near Oneida Lake, about sixty miles away, with twenty-three acres of land. In 1847, Noyes and his disciples moved there and set up the Oneida Community.

What followed was a typical American success story — success preceded by disappointment and hard work. There were only two log houses, a log hut and an old sawmill; the disciples were obliged to sleep in garrets and outhouses for another twelve years. There were many hardships until an inventor called Sewell Newhouse joined the community; he saved it from bankruptcy by inventing a steel trap which the community proceeded to manufacture. They made travelling bags, satchels, preserved fruit and silk, and their workmanship made them widely known. They acquired more land and more people joined them. Two years after the community was formed, another branch was started at Brooklyn, and then others at Wallingford, Newark, Putney, Cambridge and Manlius. By 1878 there were over three hundred members. They had built a large brick house in which they all lived. They had factories, offices, a school, a carpenter's shop, barns and stables. The Mansion House — the main building — was centrally heated, with baths and labour-saving kitchens. The community also employed over two hundred workers from outside and treated them well.

The aspect that has chiefly interested posterity was the sexual innovation. Any man could propose love-making to any woman (or, indeed, vice versa) and she was free to reject him. Oddly enough, direct courtship was not allowed — a man who wanted to sleep with a woman had to approach her through the intermediary of a third person. What "male continence" (or *coitus reservatus*) meant in practice was that the man put his penis into the woman's vagina, then they lay still for anything up to an hour and a quarter. The woman was allowed to climax but the man was not expected to do so – even after withdrawal – Noyes denounced Robert Dale Owen's idea of *coitus interruptus* as "Male incontinence plus evasion". The male was supposed to stay in the woman until he lost his erection and this was believed to obviate any frustration and nervous tension. Noyes claimed that his community had a far better record of less nervous illness than the outside community, while failing to recognize that there may have been other explanations for the situation.

As a system of sexual and moral hygiene "complex marriage" seems to have been highly successful. Boys lost their virginity soon after puberty, girls somewhat later. An older person of the opposite sex was generally chosen to initiate the young – one of the aspects of "complex marriage" that horrified the "outside world", which felt a mixture of envy and moral indignation at the idea of a middle-aged man or woman being allowed to deflower a fifteen-year-old. One visitor wrote: "The majority of the old women are hideous and loathsome in appearance and it seems to me the most horrible fate in the world to be linked with them." But Noyes himself, as the father of the community (he was even known as Father Noyes), naturally had a wider freedom of choice than most – after the age of fifty-eight he fathered eight children. It is not clear whether this was accidental or intentional. The community practised eugenics – which Noyes called stirpiculture – and at one stage, twenty-four men and twenty women were selected for an experiment in selective breeding. But "accidents" also happened – on average one every eighteen months.

Accounts of the community make clear that it was not a sexual free-for-all. The women dressed modestly, looking rather like the Chinese in long white trousers covered by a skirt. Any tendency by a couple to fall in love was regarded as selfish and "idolatrous", and was discouraged by the system of "mutual criticism", which usually meant that the person to be criticized was summoned before a committee, who then detailed his or her faults. People often requested mutual criticism just as someone today might go to a psychiatrist. One historian of the movement, Mark Holloway in *Heavens on Earth* (1951) has recorded that it was also used successfully to cure physical ailments, demonstrating that Father Noyes also understood about psychosomatic illness. There was one case in which "mutual criticism" went further: when William Mills, a man in his early sixties – with an unattractive wife – tried to initiate more than his share of teenage virgins with the aid of sweets and alcohol, and as a result was hurled unceremoniously into a snowdrift.

Close attachments among children were also discouraged as selfish, which caused a certain amount of heartache. Otherwise, the children had an enviably pleasant time. They were allowed to sleep as late as they liked in the morning and there were dances, plays, pantomimes and other forms of entertainment for them. Nor were they deprived of parental affection. A mother weaned her child, then placed it in the Children's House where, until the age of three, it spent the daylight hours. After that, children also spent the night there but parents could visit them as often as they liked and take them for walks. They left the Children's House at fourteen, when they were ready for sexual initiation and to join the adult community.

The adults also had a pleasant time of it once the community was well-established. Most members were supervisors rather than workers and they could change their jobs to avoid monotony. Times of meetings, amusements and meals were also changed for the same reason. There was fishing, hunting, boating and swimming at Oneida Lake, twelve miles away, and they could visit other communities.

The only real problem was the attitude of the outside world. The American constitution allowed for religious freedom but flagrant sexual immorality was quite another thing. One of the community's chief enemies was Professor John W. Mears, of Hamilton College, who denounced it as "a Utopia of obscenity". The Presbyterian Synod of Central New York appointed a committee of seven to investigate the activities of the community, but was unsuccessful in destroying it. Eventually, the community began to decay from within. Many younger members thought that Noyes's religious doctrines were absurd; some were even agnostics (Noyes allowed members to study Huxley and Darwin). Noyes wanted to retire and appointed his agnostic son, Dr Theodore Noyes, to take his place but this caused dissension. Some members of the community even sided with the puritanical Dr Mears. Noyes finally slipped quietly away from Oneida and moved to Niagara Falls in 1876 at the age of sixty-five. It became clear that if Oneida wanted to survive, it would have to stop outraging the outside world with its sexual freedom. "Complex marriage" was abandoned; the alternatives offered were celibacy or marriage and most preferred marriage. But to try to suppress "complex marriage" was tantamount to removing one of the main foundations of the community. "The Community sank step by step into its own Dark Ages" says one historian. The old generosity of spirit vanished, so that "it was almost impossible to borrow a hammer from one's next door neighbour". In 1881, the Oneida Community was reorganized as a joint stock company, and "communism" was abandoned. Children were still educated free until they were sixteen, then they were given $200 to give them a "start in life". "An arid commercialism" replaced the old communal spirit and the community began to split up. Yet the original Oneida branch remained commercially successful.

Noyes died in 1886 still believing firmly that the community had been ordained by God; praise and violent criticism continued long after his death. One English visitor had described him as "a tall, pale man, with sandy hair and beard, grey, dreamy oyoo, good mouth, white temples and a noble forehead." But the secularist Charles Bradlaugh was to describe him as "singularly unloveable, with his protruding, stuckout lower lip, his tired satyr-like leer . . . an eccentric goatish half-inch stripe of beard running from ear to ear." Yet fifty-three young women had once signed a resolution declaring that they belonged to him as "God's true representative", and that they were perfectly happy for him to decide which of the male members of the community were to father their children. It cannot be denied that Noyes was one of the most remarkable visionaries to come out of America in the nineteenth century.

Bernard Shaw commented about Noyes that he was "one of those chance attempts at the Superman which occur from time to time in spite of the interference of man's blundering institutions." If this study has taught us anything, it is that messiahs come in all shapes and sizes and psychological types, from the genuinely inspired to the self-deluded, from saints to con men. And in just a few cases, it is virtually impossible to decide which category a messiah belongs to.

Henry James Prince

This is the dilemma that confronts us in considering the case of the Reverend Henry James Prince, one of the most remarkable preachers of the "Spirit of Love" in the nineteenth century. After graduating from theological college in 1837 – when he was twenty-six – he became curate of Charlinch, near Bridgewater, Somerset, and was soon drawing enormous crowds with his fiery sermons. He was permanently surrounded by adoring female disciples,

The Church of the Subgenius, a Texan cult and money-making organization, worships Bob "JR" Dobbs. "Bob" is a fifties father icon, pipe firmly held between perfect teeth and hair brillantined back. The only requirement of adherents, apart from a large donation, is that they immediately reject the views of all other "Subgenii", becoming heretics and forming their own sect.

and when ugly rumours reached his bishop, he was forbidden to continue preaching. He left the Church of England and began preaching in barns and open fields. One day he announced he was the prophet Elijah, and his followers accepted the revelation without question.

Prince moved to Brighton – then a fashionable resort – and became the most popular preacher of his day. With £30,000 collected from disciples, he bought an estate at Spaxton, near Bridgewater, and turned it into *Agapomene*, or the Abode of Love. Disciples who wished to join him had to sell all they had and contribute it to the community. About sixty followers, mostly women, accepted the invitation.

Unlike his American contemporary, John Humphrey Noyes, Prince did not actually preach Free Love; but he certainly practised it, regarding his female disciples as Brides of the Lord. He himself did not mind being addressed as God, and letters addressed to Our Lord God, Somerset, reached him without difficulty. One day he summoned all his disciples to the billiard room to watch a public act of worship – his intimate union with a Miss Patterson – on the settee.

When she became pregnant, Prince told his followers that there would be no birth – just as there was now no death – but when a baby arrived, he had to explain it away as a final despairing act of the Devil. Then lawsuits began to cloud his horizon. In 1860, three female followers sued for the return of nearly £6,000, and the revelation of the goings on in the Abode of Love startled and shocked Victorian England. After the case, Prince's actions became more discreet; but he continued to live happily, surrounded by his private harem, until his death, aged eighty-eight, in 1899.

Two years before his death, Prince had acquired an influential disciple: Hugh Smyth-Pigott, another spellbinding preacher. Smyth-Pigott took over the Agapomenite Church at Clapton, a suburb of London, and his sermons were soon producing the same effect as Prince's had done half a century before. On Sunday, 7 September, 1902, Smyth-Pigott announced from the pulpit that he had become divine, and that he would shortly walk on water. The next Sunday, 6,000 people waited for his arrival, cheering and booing. Showers of stones followed him back home.

Smyth-Pigott decided to move to the Abode of Love, and in 1904 he took up residence, together with his wife and a mistress, who soon bore him a child. When, in 1909, a Bishop's Court found him guilty of "immorality, uncleanness and wickedness of life", he commented: "It doesn't matter what they do. I am God", and in the following year a daughter was born to him by another disciple.

He went preaching and gathering more disciples in America and Scandinavia; when he found particularly attractive girls, they were dubbed "soul brides" and sent back to Spaxton to await his arrival. Smyth-Pigott died in 1927, disappointing the expectations of his followers, who were convinced he was immortal. One woman, who had been brought up at the Abode of Love revealed that when the Reverend Prince had died he had handed Smyth-Pigott a "Horn of Power" and authority to carry on his mission. The exact nature of this horn of power is not known, but the symbolism seems apt.

Chapter Six

Manic Messiahs and Twentieth-Century Cults

The twentieth century has witnessed an unusually rich crop of messiahs, although it must be admitted that most of them have been con men. A few of these have aroused such indignation among their disillusioned disciples that they have met a violent end.

Franz Creffield, or Joshua the Second

The man with the enormous tangled beard raised his arm above his head and cried in a deep voice: "Bring a curse, O God, on San Fransisco, on Portland, on Corvallis and on Seattle." With which, he turned and clambered on board the train from Seattle. It was the morning of 17 April, 1906. The next day, when he arrived at his destination – Newport, Oregon – his followers met him with the incredible news: San Fransisco had just been torn apart by an earthquake, and was now burning to the ground. "Yes, I knew that God would respond," said the prophet quietly.

The man's name was Franz Edmund Creffield. He spoke with a German accent, and in the year 1906 he was thirty-one years old. He enters the history of false prophets and cranky messiahs in 1903, shortly after he had been thrown out of a Salvation Army group in Corvallis, Oregon. According to the historian Arnold Toynbee, all major prophets follow a cycle of "withdrawal and return", retreating from society to the solitude of forest or desert, and returning with the Great Message finally crystallized. Franz Creffield was no exception; early in 1903 he vanished into the forests of Oregon. When he emerged, a few months later, he had grown a beard like a briar patch full of birds' nests, and his hair fell over his shoulders. He had also acquired a new name: Joshua the Second.

Like another prophet who was making a reputation at that time – Grigory Efimovich Rasputin, the "Russian monk"– Franz Creffield held a remarkable fascination for women. There the resemblance seems to end. Rasputin undoubtedly had genuine powers of thaumaturgy, or "spirit healing", and his diaries reveal that his mystical faith was deep and genuine. Creffield, on the other hand, was a born deceiver. The best that can be said for him is that he was self-deceived.

He preached his mission in Corvallis, and acquired a few dozen followers, male and female. For some reason, the males dropped out; it was their wives and daughters who remained. Joshua's religious faith became more fervent and compelling. Surrounded by adoring women, he would call upon the "full spirit" to descend on them. They would all sway and chant, clapping rhythmically, and as the excitement became hysterical, Joshua would cry: "Begone vile clothes," and start to fling his robes around the room. The women would do the same, some of them modestly stripping down to their shifts, others flinging off every stitch. Then they would all roll on the floor, moaning and crying out.

Inevitably, the men of Corvallis began to feel uneasy, and some of the more respectable wives left. Joshua had announced that he was seeking for a woman who would become the Second Mother of Christ: he, of course, was to be the father. He searched conscientiously; many candidates were rigorously tested, and if the Holy Spirit finally indicated that none was suitable, they at least had the satisfaction of knowing they had been engaged in the Lord's work.

This quest for the Second Mother took place on Kiger Island, in the middle of a river, and throughout the summer the prophet and his followers held prayer meetings by night and danced naked in the woods by day. When the winter came, Joshua moved back into Corvallis, into the home of a man named O.P. Hunt, whose daughter Maude was one of the prophet's warmest admirers. A notice over the door said: "No Admittance Except on God's Business."

The prayer meetings finally aroused so much hostility that Joshua was summoned to the courthouse, together with his chief male disciple, Brother Brooks, for a sanity hearing. He was found sane, but advised to leave town. He ignored the suggestion, and went back to the Hunts' house. Then someone began to circulate photographs that had been taken on Kiger Island. They showed naked women — most of them recognizable as Corvallis housewives — romping in the bushes.

On 4 January, 1904, a deputation of male citizens called on the prophet, escorted him to the edge of town, tarred and feathered him, and turned him loose. He was found by Mrs Hunt and her daughter Maude and brought back home; shortly afterwards, he married Maude. But he soon felt the old compulsion to continue with the Lord's work. He went to Portland to visit one of his chief female disciples. One day, the lady's husband found the prophet performing the Lord's work without his trousers on. He took out a warrant for adultery. Joshua's angry father-in-law offered $150 for his capture, but Joshua could not be found.

Three months later, a child ran under the Hunt house — which was built clear of the ground — looking for a lost ball. He saw a bearded man dressed in a blanket, and ran out yelling. The police were called, and Joshua was dragged out. It seemed that he had been living under the house since he fled from Portland, supplied with food by his wife and her mother. In court, he admitted adultery with the Portland disciple, but explained that he could not be judged by secular law; after all, Jesus had often broken the Sabbath. He was sentenced to two years in jail, but was released after fifteen months.

His ex-wife Maude, now divorced, was living in Seattle with a brother, Frank, and sister-in-law. Joshua wrote to her, asking her to re-marry him. She agreed, and they were joined again in Seattle. The brother and sister-in-law were deeply impressed by the prophet — so much so that when Joshua ordered them to sell their home and worldly goods, and move with him to a "Garden of Eden" near Newport, Oregon, they did so without hesitation. It was as he left Seattle that Joshua pronounced the curse that "caused" the San Francisco earthquake.

Once established in his Eden, facing the Pacific Ocean just south of Waldport, the prophet sent word to former disciples in Corvallis, including a pretty girl named Esther Mitchell. Without hesitation, half the female population of Corvallis left home and streamed towards Eden. One husband rushed after his wife, pausing only to buy a revolver and cartridges.

As he reached the ferryboat across Yaquina Bay, he saw the prophet standing on deck surrounded by disciples; he pointed the revolver, and pulled the trigger five times. Nothing happened. When the outraged husband examined the pistol, he discovered the shop had sold him rimfire cartridges for a centre-fire gun, but the female disciples were not surprised; *they* knew Joshua was immortal.

All the same, the prophet could see that he was courting danger if he remained in Eden during the next week or so. The sensible course would be to allow the husbands to simmer down. As they converged on Eden, Joshua and

Maude disappeared. George Mitchell, brother of the prophet's favourite disciple Esther, reasoned that they would probably be making for Seattle again. He tracked them there on 7 May, 1906. At eight o'clock that morning, Joshua was looking in the window of Quick's Drug Store in First Avenue, while Maude was weighing herself on a machine. George Mitchell stepped up to the prophet, placed a gun against his ear, and pulled the trigger. Joshua collapsed without even turning his head. Maude flew at Mitchell, screaming. When a policeman came running up, she told him: "That is my husband Joshua. He will rise in three days."

But Joshua stayed dead, and Mitchell was tried for his murder. The defence argued that Joshua was "a degenerate of the worst sort". The jury agreed, particularly when Mitchell stated in court that Joshua had taken the virginity of *both* his sisters. George Mitchell was acquitted. His sister Esther listened impassively.

On 12 July, 1906, George Mitchell stood at King Street station, waiting to take the train home. His brother Fred saw Esther standing nearby, and asked her to come and speak to George. Esther walked over to the rest of the group, and as they moved towards the ticket barrier drew a small revolver from under the folded coat on her arm. She placed it against George's ear and pulled the trigger. Like Joshua, he collapsed without a word.

Esther Mitchell and Maude Creffield were both held — they admitted planning George's murder together. Maude took strychnine in prison; Esther was tried, but found not guilty by reason of insanity, and was committed to the Washington State Asylum. Three years later she was released, looking very thin and ill, and died at the home of friends shortly afterwards. She was just twenty.

One problem, of course, is that all "messiahs" are, by definition, persons of high dominance, and persons of high dominance are usually highly sexed. This is as true in the case of female as well as male messiahs — the best illustration being the career of a woman who was often called "the world's most pulchritudinous evangelist".

The Downfall of Aimée Semple McPherson

She was born Aimée Elizabeth Kennedy, on a small farm in Canada, near Ingersoll, Ontario, on 9 October 1890. Her mother, a highly dominant woman, had been a Salvation Army lass until she married a devout farmer many years her senior. Aimée, like her mother, had a determined character, and there was a great deal of conflict between them in her childhood. Minnie Kennedy — later known as "Ma" — found marriage to her elderly husband boring and frustrating and took it out on her family.

At the age of seventeen Aimée fell in love with a young English evangelist named Robert Semple and married him, in spite of her mother's objections. Semple intended to become a missionary and apparently felt that she would make an ideal wife. She joined her husband in his evangelist activities in Chicago, then they went to England to see his parents. But when they arrived in Hong Kong, where he intended to begin his missionary work, Semple was stricken with fever and died in the English hospital. Aimée gave birth to a girl soon afterwards. The China mission provided funds to send her back to America.

She joined her parents, who had moved to New York, tried life on the farm in Canada, then returned to New York and married a grocery clerk named Harold McPherson, by whom she had a son. Marriage bored her and within eighteen months she was on the move again, following the only profession she knew — that of evangelist. In Canada, she attracted a crowd by standing on a chair at a street corner, her eyes closed and her arms raised in prayer. As the crowd waited in silent expectation, Aimée suddenly opened her eyes and yelled, "Follow me!" and rushed to the revival hall. Once the crowd was in she shouted, "Shut the doors. Don't let anyone out."

For the next few years, it was a rather discouraging routine of travelling around the country in a battered old car with a tent in the back. Her mother joined her and took the collections. Aimée preached the literal truth of every word in the Bible and the personal return of Jesus Christ. Slowly, she acquired a following. She began to hire lecture halls. Then, in 1917, at the age of twenty-seven, she made the momentous decision to head for California. In her old car, with her mother and two children, she made her way slowly across the country.

Aimée was not, in fact, "pulchritudinous"; her features were too heavy, and her legs were like those of a Welsh dresser (so she always wore long skirts). But by the usual standards of female evangelists, she was a welcome change. Within a week of arriving in Los Angeles, she was able to rent the Philharmonic Auditorium, which held over 3,000 people. Suddenly she was a celebrity. The rich contralto voice could hold the multitudes. On a new wave of confidence, she travelled to Canada, New Zealand and Australia. It seems to have dawned on her that American sales techniques could be used to sell religion. Back in California, this time in San Diego, she scattered evangelical tracts from an aircraft and held meetings in a boxing arena.

It was in San Diego that Aimée suddenly became far more than a successful preacher. San Diego was full of old and retired citizens and the suicide rate and the statistics for mental and physical illness were far higher than in the rest of California. At an outdoor meeting in Organ Pavilion, in Balboa Park, a middle-aged paralytic rose from her wheel chair in front of 30,000 people and took a few halting steps.

Suddenly, hundreds of people were hobbling towards the platform, tears streaming down their faces, praising the Lord and Aimée Semple McPherson. The next day, everyone in San Diego was talking about the miracle.

Aimée embarked on another triumphant tour of the Pacific coast. Then she realized it was time to stop moving around like a travelling showman. She would build a temple in Los Angeles. In 1923, Los Angeles was not the world's most sprawling city; it was still an enormous village, full of country folk. They welcomed the idea of an evangelical temple, and contributed generously. On 1 January 1923, trumpets blared, and Aimée unveiled the floodlit, electrically rotating cross that formed the heart of the Angelus Temple; by night it could be seen fifty miles away. The Temple, and Sister Aimée's house next door, had cost about $1½ million. The Temple had a seating capacity of 5,000, a broadcasting station, a theological seminary, an enormous organ, and a "Miracle Room" full of discarded crutches. Groups of disciples engaged in non-stop prayer, participating in relays. Aimée, with a genius that owed something to Hollywood (and to which Billy Graham undoubtedly owes some of his own methods), held pageants with music, picture-shows of the Holy Land, and dramatized sermons, all accompanied by a vast choir. Her neighbour Carey McWilliams remarked felicitously that, "Aimée kept the Ferris wheels and merry-go-rounds of religion turning night and day." At the end of her sermons, she asked sinners to come forward to be saved; as the lights were lowered, and soft music soothed the audience, hundreds rose to their feet and moved down the aisles. Then Aimée would shout, "Turn on the lights and clear the one-way street for Jesus," and suddenly the music would turn into a brazen blare. Aimée was one of the earth's great showmen. For sheer entertainment her meetings surpassed anything that could be seen in the cinemas.

Cults and Fanatics

It was in 1925 that a new radio operator took over the Temple's radio station. His name was Kenneth G. Ormiston and he had a soothing, cultivated voice. At first, Aimée spoke to him only over the headphones; then they met by the Temple steps and she drove him home to his wife. But soon Ormiston was no longer hurrying home to his wife once the programmes were over. Instead, he went to a room in the Ambassador Hotel, where Sister Aimée was waiting. In 1926 Aimée went on a visit to the Holy Land, financed by "love offerings" from her followers. Ormiston was absent from California during this period, although it is not known for certain whether he travelled with Aimée. She was back in Los Angeles in May 1926, and continued her clandestine meetings with Ormiston in various hotels. On 14 May Ormiston rented a cottage in Carmel, told the landlord that he would be returning with his "invalid wife", and went back to Los Angeles.

Four days later, Aimée disappeared. She had gone to the beach at Venice for a swim. She sat in a beach tent, working on sermon notes, and after a while, she sent her secretary off on some errand. When the secretary returned, Aimée had vanished. Her mother proclaimed from the steps of the Temple, "She is with Jesus — pray for her." For the next thirty-two days, her followers mounted a frantic search. Aircraft flew close to the waves; men in diving suits looked for her body on the ocean floor. Two followers committed suicide — a young man yelled "I'm going after her" and leapt into the sea. Aimée's mother had flowers scattered from an aircraft on the spot. A collection of $36,000 was taken for a memorial.

On 27 May, a newspaper mentioned that Ormiston had also vanished; his wife had reported him missing. Further probing by reporters revealed that he had also been absent when Aimée was in the Holy Land. As all Los Angeles began to buzz with indecent rumour and speculation, Ormiston strolled into the search headquarters, denied all knowledge of Aimée's disappearance and vanished again.

The police of California began to suspect that there might be a connection between Aimée and Ormiston, and that if they could find one they would find the other. Suddenly the search was intensified. On the morning of 29 May Ormiston called at a Salinas garage, near Carmel, to collect his car; he was accompanied by a woman, and later that day, they registered as "Mr and Mrs Frank Gibson" at a hotel in St Luis Obispo. That night their car was stopped by a suspicious newspaper reporter. Ormiston turned and headed back towards San Francisco. Five days later, on 23 June 1926, a resident of a cottage in Agua Prieta, just across the Mexican border from Douglas, Arizona, was awakened by a knocking at the door, to be confronted by a woman who claimed she had been the victim of a kidnapping. It was Aimée.

Her story was that she had been kidnapped by two men and a woman — Rose, Steve and Jake. She had been taken to a shack in Mexico and had eventually escaped. When she returned to Los Angeles, 30,000 people were waiting at the station and she was carried to her car through lanes of flowers. Her followers showed a tendency to forgive and forget, and the rest of the world might have done the same, if Aimée had not tried quite so hard to prove her innocence.

She kept asking what the police were doing to find the kidnappers and issued challenges over the radio. A grand jury declared that there was no evidence to indict anyone. Soon after that, someone tracked down her "love nest" in Carmel. Ormiston, who was still in hiding, sent an affidavit stating that although he had stayed in the cottage with a woman who was not his wife, that woman was not Aimée. This seemed to be confirmed when a woman announced that the lady in question was her sister; Aimée publicly declared herself vindicated. But when the lady proved to be wanted by the police for passing bad cheques, the Press once again showed a disposition to regard Aimée as an adulterous woman who had decided to brazen it out. Another grand jury was convened; this time, a follower of Aimée's vanished to the lavatory with a major piece of evidence – a scrap of paper found in the "love nest" with Aimée's writing on it – and flushed it down the toilet. The grand jury was dismissed. Finally, Aimée was charged with conspiring with others to obstruct justice. She raised a "fight the Devil fund" of $¼ million, explaining to her followers that she was being crucified by the forces of evil. The evidence against her looked overwhelming; chamber-maids testified about her sessions in hotel rooms with Ormiston and the hotel registers left no doubt about it. She was identified as the "Mrs McIntyre" of the Carmel "love nest", and the cheque-bouncing lady who had supported Ormiston's story now admitted she had been paid by Aimée, who had carefully coached her in her story. And yet, in spite of all this, District Attorney Asa Keyes, suddenly moved to dismiss the case against her – there was talk of a $30,000 bribe. (Keyes was later sentenced to prison for corruption in office.) Aimée announced that the Lord had rescued her and settled down to writing her autobiography, *In the Service of the King*, in which she repeated the kidnapping story.

Soon after this, Aimée set out on another lecture tour; this time the subject was her own life and she expected her audiences to pay for admission. To her surprise, few people seemed inclined to do this. It was the same when she went on a European tour in 1928. The faithful continued to regard Sister Aimée as a saint and a wronged woman, but the general public seemed to regard her with a cynical amusement. Her publicity stunts, her public quarrels (with her mother, among others) and her law suits began to bore even the American Press. She chartered a liner for a crusade to the Holy Land but only a hundred followers turned up. For this occasion, Aimée had her chestnut hair bleached to blonde; her mother was indiscreet enough to mention that she had also had her face lifted and this alienated more of the faithful than the kidnapping escapade. In 1931, she decided to ignore her own teaching on divorce — she had always insisted that no divorced person should remarry during the lifetime of the other partner — and married an overweight radio announcer named Dave Hutton. Two days after the wedding, another woman sued Hutton for $200,000 for breach of promise. When the case was tried, Hutton was ordered to pay $5,000. But when she heard the news, Aimée fainted and fractured her skull on the flagstone of the courtyard. She went to Europe to recuperate. Hutton sent her a telegram: "Take your time, honey . . . Daddy wants a well woman." But she and Hutton never lived together again.

During the remainder of her life, she was sued fifty-five times in the courts of Los Angeles for unpaid bills, broken contracts, slander and other charges. There were a number of successful suits by relatives of Temple followers who had left their money to Aimée. She was as flamboyant as ever and as she grew older, her style in clothes became increasingly girlish, but the world had ceased to be interested in her.

On the morning of 27 September 1944, Aimée Semple McPherson was found unconscious in her hotel room in Oakland, California, with sleeping capsules scattered around her on the floor; she died later in the day. It was never established whether she had taken an overdose deliberately or accidentally.

Krishna Venta

In 1911, precisely one century after the birth of the Reverend Prince, another Messiah, Francis Pencovic, was

The Flat Earth Society flourished in Britain until the early 1970s, when Samuel and Lillian Shenton, its last active exponents died. The belief of the Society, that the earth is self-evidently not a sphere, has been around far longer than the scientifically sanctioned opposing view. The Flat Earthers' arguments tend to centre around the "fact" that if our planet was indeed a fast-rotating ball, we would all fly off it into space. Furthermore they stress that The Bible portrays the earth as flat. In order to promote their views, Flat Earthers have always been quite prepared to fight scientists on their own territory. Throughout the nineteenth century, British planists (Flat Earthers) and globularists (round earthers) had experimental showdowns, complete with impartial observers, along a six-mile stretch of canal known as the Bedford Level. The results were often disturbing for orthodox science. In one experiment a fifteen foot square blanket was hung from a bridge spanning the canal. Meanwhile, six miles down the straight waterway at another bridge, an observer attempts to focus his telescope upon the blanket. Globularist science dictates that the curvature of the earth over six miles should result in the observer not being able to see the blanket at all. However, a photo taken through the telescope revealed not only the entire blanket, but its reflection in the water below.

The first photographs of earth from space should have convinced the Flat Earthers of their error, but they had a ready explanation: the entire space programme was a sham, Arthur C. Clarke had been hired to script the moon landing. The Americans had been given the role of space race winners at a Top Secret meeting with the Soviets, in return for handing over Cuba without any fuss.

The Flat Earth Society still exists in America, crusading against the heathen globularist conspiracy.

---

born in America. Up to the time of World War II, he had a curious and chequered career as a boilermaker, shipyard worker and dishwasher, and had served jail sentences for burglary, larceny, passing dud cheques, not supporting his wife, and sending a threatening letter to Roosevelt.

It was during the war, when he was a conscientious objector, that he organized a cult called The Fountain of the World, followed by the initials WKFL (wisdom, knowledge, faith and love). When he came out of the army he changed his name to Krishna Venta, adopted flowing oriental robes, and explained that he had been born in a valley in Nepal.

He had visited Rome as long ago as AD 600 — although, on a more recent visit, the Pope's guards had turned him away — and had been "teleported" to America in 1932. The cult, with a hundred or so members, settled in Ventura County, California, near Box Canyon. According to Krishna Venta, America would be shaken by a Communist revolution in 1965, and in 1975 he and his 144,000 followers would take over the country.

On 9 December, 1958, two disgruntled ex-followers, Ralph Miller and Peter Kamenoff, called on Krishna Venta in his San Fernando Valley retreat, and demanded that he confess that his messianism was basically a cloak for sexual promiscuity — their own wives having been among the Messiah's "brides". When Krishna declined to confess, one of the men opened a canvas bag — and a tremendous explosion blew the "monastery" apart, killing a dozen people and injuring many more. In a pickup truck near-by, police found a tape recording made by the two "avengers", listing the prophet's misdemeanours, and declaring: "He isn't Christ, only a man." The words could serve as the epitaph of manic messiahs in general.

Brother Twelve

With Brother Twelve — whose real name was Edward Arthur Wilson — we again encounter the paradox of a messiah who cannot be dismissed entirely as a self-deceiver. Born in 1878 in Birmingham, England, Wilson was the son of "Irvingites". Edward Irving was a Scottish minister who was appointed to the Caledonian Church in London's Hatton Garden in 1822; convinced that the Second Coming was imminent, he induced in his congregation tremendous transports of religious fervour. When, in 1830, they offered up prayers for some "sign" or miracle, his congregation began "speaking in tongues" — that is, in strange languages, sometimes gobbledegook, but sometimes foreign languages with which they were unfamiliar. The "voices" told Irving that he was to be the new Isaiah, and that in forty days time, he would have the power to work miracles. But the forty days passed, and the miraculous power failed to descend. General disillusion followed; in 1833 he was dismissed, and in the following year died of tuberculosis.

As to Edward Wilson, born almost half a century later, he had been "in touch with super-physical beings" from an early age, but this did not prevent him from going to sea and working as a "blackbirder" — transporting kidnapped negroes to Turkey where they were sold as slaves. In 1912 he deserted his wife and children and became a wanderer. And twelve years later, at the age of forty-six, he found himself in a village in the south of France. On 19 October, 1924, he woke up and saw a "Tau" — a cross with a circle on top — suspended at the end of the bed. Thinking it was some kind of after-image, he closed his eyes and looked again; now there was also a five pointed star below it. Slowly, they faded away. But as he lay in the silence, he heard a faraway voice, "clear and wonderfully sweet", which told him that he had been a pharoah in Egypt (the Tau, or ankh, is the Egyptian symbol of life), and ordered him to prepare his heart for illumination.

In the following year, he began to practise "automatic writing", whose author identified himself as a "Master of Wisdom", a spiritual being who, according to the teaching of Madame Blavatsky (founder of the Theosophical Society), is part of a Great White Lodge whose purpose is to guide human destiny. The result was a book called *The Three Truths*. This Master gave Wilson the name "Brother Twelve". When he sent an article called "The Shadow" to the *Occult Review* in London, it was immediately accepted, and when it appeared in 1926, it created a considerable stir. Wilson foretold that a new age would begin in 1975, but that before that the world would have to struggle through an abyss of horror — a prophecy that was, on the whole, remarkably accurate.

In May 1926, at the time of the General Strike, Wilson went to London, and called on the *Occult Review*. The editor was so impressed by him (Wilson was a small man with a pointed beard, twinkling eyes, and a manner of self-evident sincerity) that he accepted a book called *The Message*, and lost no time in printing it. As its fame spread, Brother Twelve began to acquire disciples. In January 1927 he informed them, (through a "general letter") that he had been ordered by the Master to go to Canada.

Cults and Fanatics

In Ottawa, Wilson lectured to a packed meeting of the Theosophical Society, where he announced that the Masters had ordered him to form an "Aquarian Foundation", and to prepare for important Work. The talk was received with enthusiasm, and dozens of members announced their eagerness to join. It was the same when he lectured in Toronto, where — to the disgust of the Theosophical Society — crowds of members signed up. In Windsor, Ontario, his charm won over a publisher who agreed to act as intermediary between the messiah and his growing audience. In Vancouver he was met off the boat by another admirer, a lawyer, and was soon living in a small rented house and selecting members for the governing board of the Aquarian Foundation (seven of them, including himself).

Appeals for funds brought a flood of donations to build a Center in Nanaimo, British Columbia. This was run by Wilson and his common-law wife Elma. Their aim, he told members, was to fight the Empire of Evil that had been engineering catastrophes for mankind since ancient times — it had caused the downfall of Rome, and its latest effort was Bolshevism. Brother Twelve also shared with Hitler the conviction that the Jews were part of an international communist conspiracy. But his detestations were impartial, and included the Roman Catholic Church.

As the money poured in, Wilson decided to buy four hundred acres on nearby Valdes Island, and build an "ashram". He also made a determined attempt to become a political force, sending his representatives to talk to US senators, and publishing pamphlets urging the importance of forming a "Third Party", to be called the PPL, or Protestant Protective League. But the attempt to gain the support of a minority group called the Prohibition Party foundered at a Chicago convention in 1928, and Wilson reluctantly relinquished his political ambitions.

When he returned to the Center he took with him a mistress he had acquired on the train journey, Myrtle

Baumgartner. But she was quickly hustled off to Valdes Island where — Wilson told his closest confidants — she would give birth to a child who would be the new Christ. When the other disciples found out about her, there were murmurs of indignation — the first sign of the dissension that would destroy Brother Twelve's empire. They even refused to be convinced when he told them that he and Myrtle had been married in ancient Egypt. Elma Wilson — the discarded wife — was sent off to Switzerland to organize another Foundation. But her rival's days were numbered — after two miscarriages, she was also sent packing.

Meanwhile, an article in the Foundation newsletter expounding Brother Twelve's inspired revelations on "spiritual marriage" caused even more hostility. A few days later, the other six "Governors" told Brother Twelve that they had decided to dissolve the Foundation.

Ironically, it was Wilson's talent for organization that had proved to be his Achilles' heel. The disciples had worked and contributed money — sometimes a fortune. Naturally, they felt they had a say in what happened. Moreover, by law, the assets of the Foundation had to distributed among the seven Governors. Wilson was understandably indignant — after all, he was the founder — but at least he had recently collected another $25,000 from a rich admirer called Mary Connally.

When his treasurer, Robert England, defected, and took with him $2,800 that he considered Brother Twelve owed him in wages, the angry messiah swore out a warrant for his arrest on a charge of embezzlement. England was intercepted as he was leaving the country and jailed. Next, Wilson appointed four of his supporters to the now depleted Board of Governors, so he was able to outvote the remaining four. These promptly obtained an injunction freezing the $45,000 assets of the society.

Brother Twelve was becoming paranoid. Disciples noted that he had changed for the worse, and attributed this to the fact that after he had taken the "Sixth Initiation", Brother Twelve had come under the influence of a Black Adept on the spiritual plane. When Robert England was set free by the court, Wilson was furious; soon after that, England vanished, leaving all his effects behind. There is no proof that Brother Twelve had anything to do with his disappearance, but it remains a distinct possibility. At this time, Brother Twelve was found not guilty of appropriating $13,000 of the society's funds.

On 6 December, 1928, Brother Twelve gave a demonstration of what certainly looked like magical powers. An ex-disciple was suing him for $450 in back-wages. As one witness stood up in the box, he began to shake, and crashed to the floor. At the same time, several people at the back of the courtroom fainted. And when the prosecuting lawyer rose to his feet a few minutes later, he stared blankly in front of him, then began to stammer. He finally managed to gasp: "This is ridiculous, but I've forgotten what I was going to say." He shuffled back to his seat looking puzzled and bewildered.

The judge awarded a verdict in favour of Brother Twelve. But there was a general feeling that his days were numbered. And when one of his followers was arrested for raping a cinema usherette, newspapers predicted that his career was finished.

Ignoring these prophecies, Brother Twelve and the remaining faithful disciples set up a colony on Valdes Island, where a millionaire disciple named Roger Painter came to join him, bringing a red headed volatile woman named Mabel Skottowe. She and Wilson soon became lovers; Painter beat her brutally, and was ordered to leave. Mabel changed her name to "Madame Zee", and moved in with the messiah. But her bad temper — she carried a riding crop and used it unsparingly on the disciples — caused mutterings of rebellion. By now Wilson had purchased the neighbouring De Courcy Island, which had a harbour, and Mary Connally also presented him with a 160-acre property in San Bernardino, California.

When Wilson and Madame Zee moved to De Courcy Island, leaving the disciples behind, real disaffection began to set in. The disciples were expected to work long hours at building and gardening, and many of them looked forward to the day when they had enough money to leave. When he learned about this, Wilson preached an impassioned sermon about greed and treachery, and cowed them into handing over their savings.

Towards the end of 1929, Brother Twelve and Madame Zee took a year-long holiday in Europe. The island dwellers were glad to see them back — until they realized that Brother Twelve was more paranoid than ever. There were sudden and unprovoked "purges" of disciples, and when his "wife" Elma returned from her proseletysing expedition in Switzerland, she was forbidden to rejoin the colony. Even Wilson's benefactress Mary Connally was made to do domestic chores and farm work.

Brother Twelve seemed to be developing his own brand of sexual mysticism; he ordered disciples to "pair up", because sex was part of the process of "initiation". One new female disciple, Isona Supelveda, became his mistress, but was upset when her thirteen year old daughter was raped by one of the males. Another daughter had to flee in the middle of the night from the middle-aged man who had been assigned to be her lover. Brother Twelve took in their attractive fourteen year old son Dion and allegedly seduced him. When Wilson grew tired of Isona, she fled the colony and reported the rape to the police. That night, Dion stole a speedboat from the mainland and tried to return to Brother Twelve — he declared later that he had been hypnotized and ordered to return at whatever cost. (One disciple was to describe how she had seen Madame Zee exercise "mental power" over Dion; the boy was running towards Brother Twelve's cabin when Madame Zee stared after him and mentally ordered him to stop; Dion stopped in his tracks – an episode that suggests that Madame Zee may have been responsible for the problems in court.) But the rape charge was dropped, and, incredibly, the Sepulveda family returned to the island.

In the following year, 1932, an increasingly paranoid Wilson ordered the disciples to stop construction work, and to start building fortifications. He also purchased a case of carbines and some ammunition. But the seige he expected – the state government was considering criminal charges – never materialized. Instead, some bewildered and exhausted disciples fled to the mainland, while others presented Wilson with a letter telling him that they were at the end of their tether. Wilson flew into a rage, then decided to cast off the rebels; he began taking them back to the mainland in small boatloads. Those ejected from Eden included Mary Connally.

This was the last straw. The homeless ones went to a local law firm and instituted proceedings. In April 1933, Mary Connally was awarded $26,500, and another litigant, Alfred Barley (one of the earliest disciples) $14,232.

But it was too late. Brother Twelve and Madame Zee had already absconded with the cash. They moved to a farmhouse in Devon, then to Neuchatel in Switzerland. And on 7 November, 1934, Wilson died in his apartment there. Madame Zee had him cremated, then left Neuchatel. With the remainder of Brother Twelve's fortune (about $400,000), she seems to have spent her remaining years in comfort in luxury hotels.

The defectors in Vancouver refused to believe the news – they were certain that Wilson had "fabricated" his death. But in spite of a number of alleged sightings, Brother Twelve was never to reappear.

In 1991, his amazing history was reconstructed from memories of disciples by Vancouver writer John Oliphant in a book called *Brother Twelve*. It is probably the most remarkably detailed case history of a "false messiah" that has ever been compiled.

The Ku Klux Klan

During the chaos and maladministration that followed the end of the American Civil War in 1865, the social order in the defeated southern states was effectively turned upside-down. Former slaves were not only given the vote, they were given virtual freedom to take revenge on their old masters.

Gangs of ex-slaves and opportunists from the North (nicknamed "Carpetbaggers") pillaged, raped and murdered almost under the noses of the occupying Federal troops. Where punishment took place it was often ludicrously light and the whites grumbled that there was one law for "niggers" and another for "decent white folks". Into this gap in the justice system stepped former General Nathan Bedford Forrest and his Klansmen.

Forrest (who had distinguished himself during the war by ordering the massacre of over 200 surrendered black Union troops at Fort Pillow in April, 1864) told the Klansmen to dress themselves and even their horses in white shrouds; thus to convince the superstitious and poorly educated blacks that they were the avenging ghosts of Confederate soldiers.

The Klan saw themselves as modern knights, dedicated to the Southern code of honour. Indeed, in the beginning, they made some effort to catch the real offenders and the beatings generally out-numbered the lynchings, but their very popularity eventually brought about their collapse.

By the 1870's, the Klan membership had swelled to tens of thousands and Forrest's "secret army" was totally unmanagable. He watched with growing disgust as Klan posses looted and butchered almost indiscriminately among the black communities across the South and, along with his staff, he resigned in 1872. With the change in the political climate at the time (*ie* the North selling-off the black's rights in return for economic agreement with the South), the Klan's reason for existence vanished and it soon died out. It did not, however, stay dead.

In 1915, coinciding with the release of D.W. Griffith's apparently pro-Klan movie, *Birth of a Nation*, an Atlanta Methodist preacher, "Colonel" William Joseph Simmons, started to agitate for a rebirth of the "noble order". He received widespread support and the new Ku Klux Klan soon had a rocketing membership. This time though, it's interests were not in the restoration of social order, but the instigation of racial hatred.

Simmons and his fellows' vitriol was not just aimed at the blacks; Catholics, Jews, non-Americans and all critics of the Ku Klux Klan were also attacked. This broad appeal-base swelled the movement to hundreds of thousands throughout the First World War and on into the next two decades. At the same time, its leaders became stunningly rich by skimming the Klan's funds. By the 1930 s, the Klan was one of the most powerful financial institutions in the USA.

The cost to human life exacted by this hate machine was appalling. The actual number of lynchings and burnings is unknown – partially due to cover-ups by Klan-friendly police departments – but other atrocities, deliberately publicised by the Klan, were also common. Whippings, shootings, mutilations, rapes and brandings with the letters "KKK" were common throughout the 1920's and 30's. The Government seemed powerless or unwilling to stop the persecutions.

Then, with the coming of the Second World War, membership started to drop off. In an attempt to revive their fortunes, the Klan leaders forged an alliance with the Nazi American Bund. When the Bund was denounced as un-

American and dispanded the Klan tried to erase its links with the group, but it was too late; the mud stuck and membership crashed. In 1944, the Internal Revenue Service charged the Klan with failure to pay massive back taxes; this was the final straw. On 23rd April, 1944, the Klan leaders officially dissolved the movement; but, again, it refused to die.

Separate groups of Ku Klux Klansmen managed to keep the ugly dream alive throughout the 1940's and 50's. In the 1960's the movement received a boost during the civil rights troubles, but stood little chance of a full revival. The mood of the country had changed, and it was now the racists who were looked upon with distrust and loathing.

In the 1970's and 80's the Klan hung-on, but has undergone several important changes. It's new emphasis is on religious fundamentalism (which was always a part of its belief, but never the backbone, which had always been racism) and post-nuclear Survivalism. The new creed predicts that the forces of Satan (led by Jews, Communists and non-whites) will cause a nuclear Armaggedon which will be followed by a war between the powers of Good and Evil. In the preparation for this day, the modern Ku Klux Klan has set-up several paramilitary training camps in the southern states.

Charles Manson

A former Brother Twelve disciple alleged in court that Wilson had ordered him to kill one of his enemies by black magic, but that he had refused. In that respect, at least, Wilson had a less malign influence than Charles Manson, the "hippie" messiah of the 1960s.

Manson was born in Cincinatti in 1934, the son of a fifteen-year-old girl who had become pregnant by her seventeen-year-old boyfriend. His mother was reported by neighbours to be "loose". "She ran around a lot, drank, got in trouble." She also vanished for days at a time. When Charlie was five, she was sentenced to five years in prison for armed robbery. Out again in 1942, she tried to have her son taken into a foster home, but none were available; at twelve, he was sent to a "caretaking institution" for boys in Indiana. After running away several times — his mother did not want him at home — he was arrested for burglary; escaping from custody he committed a series of burglaries and armed robberies, for which he was sent to a reform school when he was thirteen. A parole officer later said: "Charlie was the most hostile parolee I've ever come across." Small and not particularly strong, Manson was nevertheless a highly dominant person who felt that his best defence was to "act tough". He also committed a number of homosexual offenses, including rape, holding a razor against the victim's throat.

Released from reformatory at twenty, he married a seventeen-year-old girl and drove her to Los Angeles in a stolen car; in March 1956, a son was born. Three months later Manson was sent to prison again for car theft. He was behind bars intermittently until 1967, when he was thirty-two.

Free once more, he drifted to San Francisco, which was then crowded with "hippies" who smoked pot and talked about flower power. For Manson, this was a revelation; the world had changed totally since 1956. Older than most of the drop-outs on Haight-Ashbury, he was soon a local "character", with his own admiring retinue of teenagers. He took full advantage of the new sexual freedom, and accumulated a kind of harem. One girl, Mary Brunner, was later described as his "favourite wife". Another, Lynn ("Squeaky") Fromme joined his menage when he found her crying by the side of the road after a family row. Yet another, Susan Atkins, later described how Manson had given her confidence by making her undress, then telling her: "Look, you're beautiful." What such girls found attractive about Manson was that he was a totally un threatening father figure, a kind of mixture of Charlie Chaplin and Christ. He liked to point out that his name meant "Man's son", and clearly thought of himself as a Christ figure.

By October 1967, Manson was tired of Haight-Ashbury, and moved with his disciples to Topanga Canyon, Los Angeles. There were about sixteen girls in the group by this time, and four men. One of the girls, Sandy Good, told him about a ranch owned by an old man named George Spahn, who was almost blind. Manson went to look at it, and Spahn allowed the hippies to stay for several weeks.

Manson's ambition was to become a pop star, like Bob Dylan; he played guitar and sang his own songs. Terry Melcher, son of the film star Doris Day, talked about a $20,000 record contract. Manson sold a song to the successful pop group, the Beach Boys, whose drummer, Dennis Wilson, allowed the "family" to move into his luxury home for a while. It suddenly began to look as if Manson might end up rich and famous too.

Another coup was persuading the owner of a small ranch near the Spahn ranch to give it to them — while they were all under the influence of drugs — in exchange for a painted tent.

But success continued to elude him, and he developed an increasing tendency to denounce civilization and all its evils. He was convinced that a nuclear holocaust was imminent and that blacks were poised to take over America. (Oddly enough, Manson was violently racist.) In October 1968, the "family" drove an old bus into Death Valley, in the Mojave desert, until the brakes burned out, then moved into a derelict farm, the Barker ranch. When winter came they moved back to Los Angeles, and Manson's next door neighbour commented that he was very opinionated and very anti-establishment, and that Manson's women said "they would give their lives for Charlie".

It seems likely that at this period, Manson's non-stop psychedelic trips began to induce intense paranoia (although even at reform school, psychiatrists had noted some paranoia). The Beatles song "Helter Skelter" provided him with a code name for the day of reckoning for the "pigs" – the bourgeoisie, the blacks and the authorities. The family began to acquire guns and knives, and two "dune buggies" – vehicles that would run on sand – one with a forged cheque and one with stolen money. In 1969, he shot a negro dope dealer named Crowe in the torso – although Crowe recovered in hospital and no questions were asked. Manson was relieved when no Black Panthers came to seek revenge.

In July 1969, a Zen Buddhist convert called Gary Hinman – who had refused to sell all he had and join the family – was held at gunpoint while the family searched his home for money. When Hinman showed fight, Manson slashed his face with a sword, half severing an ear. After that, Hinman was forced to sign over his car and bus to Manson, then stabbed twice and left to bleed to death.

The police were now harrassing the "family", who were back at the Spahn ranch – looking for stolen cars and stolen credit cards. In early August 1969, Manson told his followers: "Now is the time for Helter Skelter."

On the evening of Friday 8 August, a murder party of four left for a house in Hollywood where Terry Melcher had once lived; Manson chose it because he knew it. Tex Watson, Linda Kasabian, Susan Atkins and Patricia Krenwinkel drove to 10050 Cielo Drive, and Watson cut the telephone wires. The house had now been let to film director Roman Polanski, who was in London, and his wife Sharon Tate was giving dinner to three guests: Jay Sebring, an ex-lover, Voityck Frykowski, and his girlfriend

Abigail Foldger, who were staying. Sharon Tate was heavily pregnant.

A youth named Stephen Parent, who had been visiting the house boy, drove down the drive on his way home and called to ask the dark figures what was happening. Tex Watson shot him five times in the head. Then they broke into the house by cutting through a screen window.

Frykowski had fallen asleep on the settee under the influence of drugs; Abigail Folger had retired to bed for the same reason. Sebring was talking to Sharon Tate in her bedroom. Watson woke Frykowski up and ordered Susan Atkins to tie his hands. Sebring came downstairs asking what was happening and made a grab for the gun; Watson shot him in the lung. Then a rope was thrown over a beam and tied round the necks of Sebring, Abigail Folger and Sharon Tate. As Sebring began to struggle, Watson stabbed him several times. Frykowski began to run, and was shot in the back, then clubbed. Abigail Folger, also running, was stabbed by Patricia Krenwinkel. Out in the garden, where Linda Kasabian was keeping watch, Frykowski was stabbed to death by Watson. Then, back in the house, Watson ignored Sharon Tate's pleas for mercy and stabbed her in the breast. Finally, Susan Atkins wrote "Pig" in blood on the door, and they left.

They stripped off their bloody clothes and washed themselves with a grass sprinkler on someone's lawn; the elderly house owner came out and shooed them off, noting the number of their car as they drove away.

Later that night, Manson seems to have come to the house to make sure everyone was dead. And the next morning, the family watched with delight as news of the murders was broadcast on television.

The aim of Helter Skelter was to make whites believe that blacks were about to start a massacre, and to massacre them in turn. It seemed logical to Manson that if this was to be achieved, the murders had to be followed up as soon as possible. That evening, seven family members, all high on "acid", set out for a well-to-do area of Los Angeles, Los Feliz, and chose a house at random. But when Manson saw pictures of children through the window, he ordered them to move on to a house with an expensive car and a boat trailer outside. It was the home of a middle aged couple, Leno and Rosemary LaBianca.

The LaBiancas had gone to bed when Charles Manson walked into their bedroom with a gun and ordered them to get up. He tied them up, then went back to the car and ordered Watson, Patricia Krenwinkel and Leslie Van Houten to go into the house and kill them. He, meanwhile, would go off with the others and kill someone else.

Watson and his helpers found the LaBiancas lying quietly. Mrs LaBianca was led to a bedroom and tied with electric flex; then her husband was stabbed in the throat. When Rosemary LaBianca screamed "What are you doing to my husband?", Patricia Krenwinkel stabbed her in the back, severing her spine. Watson slashed the word "War" on LaBianca's chest while Patricia Krenwinkel stabbed both bodies with a carving fork. After it was clear the victims were dead, they scrawled "Death to pigs" and "Rise" – and a mis-spelled version of "Helter Skelter" – on the wall, then took a shower, and fed the dogs (who had watched the murders without barking, and even licked their hands). They then hitch-hiked back to the Spahn ranch where Manson was waiting. The murders he had intended to commit had been abandoned; in fact, he had left the girls in an apartment block with orders to kill a film actor, but they had deliberately knocked on the wrong door and went away again.

The slaughter created the sensation Manson had hoped for – suddenly the sale of handguns and burglar alarms soared in Los Angeles. Six days later, the stolen car used in both crimes was seized by the police – but not in connection with the murders; they had decided to swoop on the hippie commune in search of drugs, guns and stolen vehicles. Unfortunately, the man who had chased the Sharon Tate killers off his lawn failed to report the incident to the police, otherwise the case would probably have been solved immediately. Manson and twenty-four other people were arrested, but released three days later for lack of evidence.

On 26 August, less than two weeks after the murders, a Spahn ranch hand named Shorty O'Shea vanished; his body was never found, but it is believed that he was tortured and killed by the family because he had married a negro woman, and because he knew too much.

In 12 September, 1969, the family moved back to Death Valley. There they courted the attention of the police by wantonly burning a bulldozer belonging to the local rangers. Tyre tracks led them to a stolen car, and a miner told them about the family (who had made an unsuccessful attempt to kill him). On 9 October police surrounded the Barker ranch, then arrested everyone on it – mostly girls, who tried to disconcert them by removing their clothes and urinating. Manson returned to the ranch three days later, to be told about the arrests by a few girls who had escaped the raid. While he was eating, the police descended again. Manson almost escaped by hiding in a tiny cupboard under the kitchen sink, but was detected.

It was Susan Atkins, in prison in Los Angeles on suspicion of knowing something about the Gary Hinman murder, who betrayed the family. She began to drop hints to fellow prisoners about the Sharon Tate killings, and finally described them to her cellmate in detail. The cellmate reported this to another prisoner, who reported it to the police. Under questioning, Susan Atkins was soon confessing the whole story.

The trial was one of the most expensive in Los Angeles history (although in this respect it was surpassed by the trial of the Hillside Stranglers, Buono and Bianchi, ten years

In 1982, Manson was moved from a maximum
security jail to Vacaville Prison, fifty miles
northeast of San Francisco. On the night of 29
October, a guard noticed an open door in the
prison chapel, where Manson worked as a
cleaner. Manson and three other prisoners were
found there. In the attic of the chapel, a search
revealed a tape recorder, tin cutters, a hacksaw,
sandpaper, a tin of inflammable liquid, nylon
rope, and a catalogue for hot air balloons. There
was also a quantity of marijuana. Manson, it
seems, had been planning an escape bid in which
the hot air balloon would carry them over the
prison wall, and had had the catalogue sent to
him quite openly.

later). It had a slightly surrealistic air, since Manson seemed
to have no regard for normal logic, and insisted that they
were innocent because society was guilty. Asked if she
thought the killing of eight people unimportant, Susan
Atkins asked if the killing of thousands of people with
napalm was important. Manson became a hero of the
hippies, who saw him as a figure of social protest; there
can be no doubt that if he had been released, he would soon
have had as huge a following as any messiah in history.

Even after the arrests, the murders went on. Defense
attorney Ronald Hughes disappeared eight days into the
trial; his badly decomposed body was found in the desert at
about the time of the sentencing; he had strongly disagreed
with the decision of Manson's co-defendants to insist that
he was not guilty. In his book *Helter Skelter*, prosecution
attorney Vincent Bugliosi lists a dozen other murders
connected with the family, including those of two family

members believed to have killed Hughes.

On 30 March, 1970, Charles Manson, Susan Atkins, Leslie Van Houten and Patricia Krenwinkle were sentenced to death; in 1971 Watson received the same sentence. In effect, this meant life imprisonment.

In September 1975, Lynette "Squeaky" Fromme attempted to assassinate President Gerald Ford, but her gun misfired; she was sentenced to life imprisonment.

In April 1992, Manson — now housed in a maximum security prison in the San Joaquin Valley — made his eighth appeal for parole, but was turned down by the board.

The Matamoros Murders

It might seem impossible to imagine a cult leader more dangerous and inhuman than Charles Manson. But the details of the Matamoros murders — which began to emerge in mid-1989 — made it clear that Adolfo Constanzo was a serious contender for the title of America's most sadistic serial killer.

Unlike most practitioners of black magic, Adolfo Constanzo was not just an eccentric who made up his ceremonies as he went along. According to his followers, he often boasted that he had been schooled in the dark religion of Palo Mayombe from his earliest childhood. Brought up by his expatriate Cuban mother in Miami, Florida, he claimed that she was a fully trained priestess in the blood cult, and that his earliest memory was of the sacrifice of a chicken.

Palo Mayombe is the dark sister of the Santeria religion. Both originated on the west coast of Africa and were brought over by slaves sent to the Spanish plantations of Cuba. The Spaniards had insisted, on pain of death, that all slaves convert to Christianity. They were gratified when their captives appeared to do so without fuss; in fact the slaves had retained all the essentials of their old religion by associating their gods with the icons of Catholic saints. (The Spanish overlords did not mind their slaves making blood sacrifices to the holy images – they attributed it to simple, Old Testament primitivism).

Santeria (meaning literally "the saints' path") has survived as a mixture of Christianity and the old, voodoo-like African religion. Its "spells" can be used for good as well as harmful purposes and in basic attitude it most resembles the European tradition of "white magic".

Palo Mayombe, which originated in the Congo area, is less benevolent. The religion centres around the *nganga*; a caldron filled with blood, a decomposing goat's head, a roasted turtle, sacred stirring sticks and, most importantly, a human skull – preferably belonging to a violent person who died a sudden death. The confused soul of the dead person is trapped in the *nganga* and will obey the orders of the Palo Mayombe priest if kept in a state of contentment with freshly spilled blood. The "bound" spirit is said to be able to curse enemies, foretell the future and provide both magical and physical protection (even from bullets).

The purpose of a Palo Mayombe priest is to gain ultimate power in life since he or she believes that tales of an afterlife are lies. Dead spirits, they say, simply wander the material plane as if in limbo. At initiation, the new priest declares his soul to be dead and dedicates himself to the Congoese god of destruction, *Kadiempembe* "the Eater of Souls". Thus, without an eternal spirit, he has nothing to lose and may do as he will with savage freedom. Non-believers, especially Christians, are considered "animals" who should be exploited mercilessly.

The skull for the *nganga* is traditionally obtained by grave-robbing, but Adolfo Constanzo told his followers that his "Padrino", or Godfather, – the name given to high priests of the cult – had "hunted" living donors in his youth on Haiti. Constanzo intended to follow in his footsteps.

A dark, handsome youth with piercing eyes, Constanzo always made a powerful impression. When he moved to Mexico City in 1982, at the age of twenty-one, he quickly saw that, in the corrupt, superstitious atmosphere of the capital's underworld, a "padrino" could become a wealthy man . . .

He set up as a fortune-teller and soon built a reputation for uncanny accuracy. Many of the city's drug barons relied on his forecasts to decide when to send shipments across the American border. Subsequent investigation has revealed that much of his "divined" information came from corrupt officials in the Mexican drug administration – at least two of whom were his disciples.

He quickly built up a hard core of a dozen or so dedicated followers who would meet in the secret room in his luxury apartment that contained the stinking *nganga*, and enact blood sacrifices – killing chickens, goats, dogs and cats – to ensure good luck and obtain protection from the police.

Observing the huge amount of money being made by the relatively simple, uneducated drug lords, Constanzo decided to break into the protection racket. He told the head of one clan of drug dealers, Guillermo Calzada, that for a large fee he would be willing to be his in-house fortune-teller – magically protecting him and his drugs at all times. Calzada, having experienced the accuracy of Constanzo's forecasts, accepted eagerly.

Not long afterwards, Constanzo visited him and explained that in veiw of the fact it was his magic that was really doing the work, he deserved half the profits . . . Calzada refused, and Constanzo left in a rage. A few days later the padrino called Calzada and begged his forgiveness. As a reconciliation he offered to place a specially powerful protection spell of Calzada and his family. Calzada agreed and on 30 April, 1987, he, his wife, his ageing mother, his partner Jose Rolon, his secretary, his maid and his bodyguard met with Constanzo in a deserted factory.

Cults and Fanatics

All seven reappeared in the Rio Zumpango river, north of the Mexico City, several days later. They had been horribly mutilated before they were killed. Their fingers, toes, ears and, in the case of the men, genitals had been cut-off. The hearts were also missing from some of the bodies and, more significantly, the heads.

Constanzo fed the butchered remains to his *nganga*, thus gaining power over the anguished spirits of the owners, who would use ghostly toes to travel, fingers to manipulate, ears to hear, and hearts and genitals to accumulate power. These damned souls were to be his servants as he expanded his operations to the Mexico/Texas border and the town of Matamoros.

Mexico City, Constanzo had decided, was too far from the most lucrative market for drugs; the United States. Matamoros, a tourist town on the Mexican side of the Rio Grande, would be an ideal base for his own drugs empire. He told one of his most ardent followers, Federal Narcotics agent Salvador Garcia, to apply for a transfer to the border town and assess the situation. Some weeks later Garcia reported that the Hernandez family, well known locally to be drug smugglers, were having problems since the death of their leader in a gang shoot-out. His brothers were unable to run the business efficiently and were badly in need of magical assistance. Constanzo made suitable blood sacrifices for luck and travelled to Matamoros.

His method of contacting the Hernandez brothers illustrates his subtlety. He arranged a "chance" meeting with Sara Aldrete, an attractive honours student at the Brownsville College, just across the border. Sara had once dated Elio Hernandez, the boss of the family since the death of his brother, but had not seen him for years. Constanzo, after impressing her with his prophetic powers and luring her into bed, told her an old friend would soon contact her and tell her he was in trouble; she was to tell him that she had met a powerful magus who might be the answer to all his problems : . .

Sure enough, Sara bumped into Elio Hernandez in the street shortly afterwards and when he had related his woes she persuaded him to meet with Constanzo. The padrino hooked Elio with his usual skill, and soon most of the drug dealers in the family gang were attending Constanzo's blood sacrifices (Sara Aldrete was made a high priestess and was, in theory, the controller of the Matamoros branch of the cult when Constanzo was in Mexico City).

As promised, the Hernandez family business was soon flourishing under the prophetic guidance of Padrino Adolfo; the delivery runs went smoothly and the money flowed in. Then in the spring of 1988, Constanzo told them that he had a better idea than buying drugs — stealing them from small time drug runners. Using information from one of the cult members, he located a large marijuana stash, and the family helped themselves. The original owner, and the farmer on whose land it had been hidden, was taken to an orchard and shot in cold blood.

It was the family's first experience of Constanzo's ruthlessness and they were shocked, nevertheless, they swallowed their revulsion. Now they were implicated in murder, they could be introduced into the darker secrets of Palo Mayombe. They were soon convinced that every time they made an important drugs run or needed to avert misfortune they should make a ritual human sacrifice.

Between May, 1988 and March, 1989, Constanzo and his followers tortured and murdered at least thirteen people at the deserted Hernandez ranch outside Matamoros. Most of the victims were rival drugs dealers or, occasionally, lapsed members of the cult. But some victims were strangers who were kidnapped while walking along the local highway, and murdered without being asked their names. Elio Hernandez was horrified to discover one day that the fourteen-year-old boy he had just decapitated without looking at his face was, in fact, his second cousin.

All the cult's known victims at Matamoros were male – Constanzo was bi-sexual with a distinct homosexual bias. The treatment meted-out to them before they were allowed to die would have horrified an Aztec priest. The terrified victim would be beaten and kicked and then dragged into a shed that contained the sacred *nganga*. Often his extremities (such as fingers, genitals, nose and ears) would be cut-off and Constanzo would partially flay him. Then the others would be asked to leave while the padrino sodomized him. Finally, the victim would be "sacrificed" by either cutting-out his heart or lopping off the top of his head – Constanzo would often leave the death blow to one of the others to increase their complicity. The victims' severed parts, brains, heart and blood would be placed in the *nganga*. Their corpses were buried in shallow graves nearby.

It was regarded as essential that the victim should scream as he died – the soul, Constanzo believed, must be confused and terrified when it left the body, to make it easier to subjugate. Oddly enough it was this obsession that was to bring about his downfall.

In March, 1989, his henchmen kidnapped a street cocaine dealer that none of them recognized – he has never been identified – and Constanzo went to work on him. But despite all his efforts he could not make the tough little Mexican cry out, even when he skinned his upper torso. The victim died without screaming. Constanzo was un-nerved and declared the ceremony a failure. What they needed he decided was an American; someone soft, "someone who will scream".

The next victim was easy to find. At the beginning of March, Matamoros is generally packed with American "spring breakers" – mostly students from Texas attracted by cheap alcohol, pot and cocaine. The cultists simply waited until around two in the morning, found a drunk student heading back across the border, and offered him a lift. His name was Mark Kilroy, a twenty-one-year-old first year medical student from the University of Texas. Constanzo did a very thorough job on the youth and was deeply satisfied with the result. He sliced the top from the screaming American's head with a machete and dropped his brains into the *nganga*.

Now, he told his excited followers, they were unstoppable. Previously they had only had Mexican spirits to protect them on the south side of the border; now they had an American ghost to keep them safe from the Texas police. They were now, he said, effectively invisible.

But Constanzo's sadism had overreached itself this time. The disappearance of an American student in Matamoros might normally have failed to attract much attention. But Mark Kilroy was the nephew of an important US Customs Advisor and the authorities on both sides of the border were soon involved in a large scale search.

A few days after the sacrifice of Mark Kilroy, Serafin Hernandez Jnr, Elio's nephew, casually drove his pick-up truck past a queue of traffic and a police roadcheck as if they could not see him. A patrol car quietly followed this apparent madman all the way to the Hernandez ranch. They waited until he had left again and searched the place. They found evidence of the storage of drugs and had him arrested.

After a little heavy persuasion (involving the squirting of soda water spiked with tabasco up his nostrils — an agonizing but undetectable torture) he unexpectedly confessed to more shocking crimes than drug dealing. His casual confession — he still believed that the police could not defeat his padrino's magic — led them back to the ranch to the shallow graves and the *nganga* shed.

The police quickly moved to arrest all the members of the cult named in Serafin's confession, but were too late to catch the padrino and his closest associates; Constanzo and

> The religions of Santeria and Palo Mayombe are so wide-spread in Miami's Cuban population, that the Miami River has been nicknamed "the River of Chickens" by the sanitation crews that work on it. Over a three-day period in 1989, a crew dredged up two hundred headless, unplucked chickens, twenty-two beheaded ducks, and a collection of other sacrificed fauna, including cats, dogs, snakes, eels, turtles, pigeons, iguanas and pelicans.

his inner circle had already fled to Mexico City. The discoveries at the ranch worried many influential people. Constanzo had been a fashionable fortune-teller, and many of his clients were from Mexican high society. Some of these were worried simply about their reputations. Others, especially in law enforcement, were terrified that Constanzo's confession might reveal their involvement in drug trafficking. They could only pray that he would not be taken alive.

After a brief stop in the capital, Constanzo and his followers fled to the resort of Cuernavaca, fifty miles south of Mexico City. They were not, in fact, too concerned about the problem; they had a large amount of money on them and were convinced that when things cooled-down they could buy their way across the border. In fact, after three weeks, they even returned to Mexico City and hid in the apartment of a friend.

On the 5 May, a police informer reported that a woman fitting Sara Aldrete's description had been seen buying a large quantity of food, and that he had followed her to her apartment. The next day, Constanzo's lookouts spotted cars of plain-clothes policemen moving in on the apartment block. Constanzo rushed to the window and saw heavily armed policemen preparing to storm the building.

Panic reigned among the cultists. Constanzo and a henchman named Valdez — nicknamed "El Dubi" — exchanged machine-gun fire with the police, while Sara Aldrete and another lover of Constanzo's, Omar Ochoa, hid under a bed. Then the hysterical padrino started to pile wads of money into the gas stove and burnt them.

He and El Dubi continued to fire on the police until they were almost out of ammunition. Then, suddenly calm, Constanzo announced that they must all kill themselves. Taking his bodyguard/lover, Martin Rodriguez, into a walk-in closet he ordered El Dubi to shoot them. When the gunman just stared at him he slapped him and said "Do it or I'll make things tough on you in Hell." As El Dubi raised the weapon Constanzo said calmly; "Don't worry, I'll be back. Now do it." At the order Valdez sprayed them with bullets. Both died instantly.

The others were taken alive. Detailed confessions revealed that there had been fifteen murders at Matamoros, and eight in Mexico City (the eighth victim in the capital was a transvestite called Ramon Esquivel who had been tortured, murdered and his dissected body left on a public street corner). They added to a total of twenty-three "sacrifices" to the God Kadiempembe. Police later investigated the possibility that Constanzo's gang was responsible for sixteen ritual murders of children, all under the age of sixteen.

The Matamoros police had the *nganga* and the shed that contained it exorcized by a *curandero* or white witch. Then they doused the shed with petrol and burned it to the ground.

Chapter Seven

Murdering Madmen

During the 20th century the serial killer has emerged. He tends to choose his victims at random, his motive is usually sexual. Even more important is the fact that he (or she) becomes addicted to murder, exactly as if it were a drug, some even claim to be led by the voice of God.

The Yorkshire Ripper

During the second half of the 1970s, the killer who became known as the Yorkshire Ripper caused the same kind of fear among prostitutes in the north of England as his namesake in the Whitechapel of 1888.

His reign of terror began in Leeds on a freezing October morning in 1975, when a milkman discovered the corpse of a woman on a recreation ground; her trousers had been pulled down below her knees, and her bra was around her throat. The whole of the front of the body was covered with blood; pathologists later established that she had been stabbed fourteen times. Before that, she had been knocked unconscious by a tremendous blow that had shattered the back of her skull. She was identified as a twenty-eight-year-old prostitute, Wilma McCann, who had left her four children alone to go on a pub crawl. Her killer seemed to have stabbed and slashed her in a frenzy.

Three months later, on 20 January, 1976, a man on his way to work noticed a prostrate figure lying in a narrow alleyway in Leeds, covered with a coat. Like Wilma

McCann, Emily Jackson had been half-stripped, and stabbed repeatedly in the stomach and breasts. She had also been knocked unconscious by a tremendous blow from behind. When the police established that the forty-two-year old woman was the wife of a roofing contractor, and that she lived in the respectable suburb of Churwell, they assumed that the killer had selected her at random and crept up behind her with some blunt instrument. Further investigation revealed the surprising fact that this apparently normal housewife supplemented her income with prostitution, and that she had had sexual intercourse shortly before death — not necessarily with her killer. The pattern that was emerging was like that of the Jack the Ripper case: a sadistic maniac who preyed on prostitutes.

Just as in Whitechapel in 1888, there was panic among the prostitutes of Leeds, particularly in Chapeltown, the red light area where Emily Jackson had been picked up. But as no further "Ripper" murders occurred in 1976, the panic subsided. It began all over again more than a year later, on 5 February, 1977, when a twenty-eight-year-old woman named Irene Richardson left her room in Chapeltown looking for customers, and encountered a man who carried a concealed hammer and a knife. Irene Richardson had been struck down from behind within half an hour of leaving her room; then her attacker had pulled off her skirt and tights, and stabbed her repeatedly. The wounds indicated that, like Jack the Ripper, he seemed to be gripped by some awful compulsion to expose the victim's intestines.

Now the murders followed with a grim repetitiveness that indicated that the serial killer was totally in the grip of his obsession. During the next three and a half years, the man whom the press christened the Yorkshire Ripper, murdered ten more women, bringing his total to thirteen, and severely injured three more. Most of the victims were prostitutes, but two were young girls walking home late at night, and one of them a civil servant. With one exception, the method was always the same – several violent blows to the skull, which often had the effect of shattering it into many pieces, then stab wounds in the breast and stomach. In many cases, the victim's intestines spilled out. The exception was a civil servant named Marguerite Walls, who was strangled with a piece of rope on 20 August, 1979, after being knocked unconscious from behind.

One victim who recovered – forty-two-year-old Maureen Long – was able to describe her attacker. On 27 July, 1977, she had been walking home through central Bradford after an evening of heavy drinking when a man in a white car offered her a lift. As she stepped out of the car near her front door, the man struck her a savage blow on the head, then stabbed her several times. But before he could be certain she was dead, a light went on in a nearby gypsy caravan, and he drove away. She recovered after a brain operation, and described her attacker as a young man with long blond hair – a detail that later proved to be inaccurate.

Her mistake may have saved the Ripper from arrest three months later. A prostitute named Jean Jordan was killed near some allotments in Manchester on 1 October, 1977. When the body was found nine days later – with twenty-four stab wounds – the police discovered a new £5 note in her handbag. Since it had been issued on the other side of the Pennines, in Yorkshire, it was obviously a vital clue. The police checked with the banks, and located twenty-three firms in the Leeds area who had paid their workers with £5 notes in the same sequence. Among the workers who were interviewed was a thirty-one-year-old lorry driver named Peter Sutcliffe, who worked at T and W. H. Clark (Holdings) Ltd, and lived in a small detached house at 6 Garden Lane in Bradford. But Sutcliffe had dark curly hair and a beard, and his wife Sonia was able to provide him with an alibi. The police apologized and left, and the Yorkshire Ripper was able to go on murdering for three more years.

As the murders continued – four in 1977, three in 1978, three in 1979 – the police launched the largest operation that had ever been mounted in the north of England, and thousands of people were interviewed. Police received three letters signed "Jack the Ripper", threatening more murders, and a cassette on which a man with a "Geordie" accent taunted George Oldfield, the officer in charge of the case; these later proved to be false leads. The cassette caused the police to direct enormous efforts to the Wearside area, and increased the murderer's sense of invulnerability.

The final murder took place more than a year later. Twenty-year-old Jacqueline Hill, a Leeds University student, had attended a meeting of voluntary probation officers on 17 November 1980, and caught a bus back to her lodgings soon after 9 p.m. An hour later, her handbag was found near some waste ground by an Iraqi student, and he called the police. It was a windy and rainy night and they found nothing. Jacqueline Hill's body was found the next morning on the waste ground. She had been battered unconscious with a hammer, then undressed and stabbed repeatedly. One wound was in the eye – Sutcliffe later said she seemed to be looking at him reproachfully, so he drove the blade into her eye.

This was the Ripper's last attack. On 2 January, 1981, a black prostitute named Olive Reivers had just finished with a client in the centre of Sheffield when a Rover car drove up, and a bearded man asked her how much she charged; she said it would be £10 for sex in the car, and climbed in the front. He seemed tense and asked if she would object if he talked for a while about his family problems. When he asked her to get in the back of the car, she said she would prefer to have sex in the front; this may have saved her life – Sutcliffe had stunned at least one of his victims as she climbed into the back of the car. He moved on top of her, but was unable to maintain an erection. He moved off her again, and at this point, a police car pulled up in front. Sutcliffe hastily told

Cults and Fanatics

In 1985, the suicide of a man named Leonard
Lake, and the flight of his companion Charles
Ng, led the police to a house in Calaveras
County, California, and to a cache of videos
showing the sexual abuse and torture of female
victims – the number seems to have exceeded
thirty. Ex-convict Gerald Gallego and his
mistress Charlene Williams made a habit of
abducting and murdering teenage girls, who
were first subjected to an orgy of rape and
lesbian advances, all in the search for the
"perfect sex slave". In Chicago, a group of four
young men, led by twenty-seven-year-old Robin
Gecht, abducted at least fifteen women, and
subjected them to an orgy of rape and torture –
which included amputation and ritual eating of
the breasts – in the course of "satanic"
ceremonies. There was also evidence to link the
New York Killer "Son of Sam" – David
Berkowitz – who casually shot strangers in cars
– with a satanic cult. It was hard to imagine how
human depravity could go any further.

the woman to say she was his girlfriend. The police asked
his name, and he told them it was Peter Williams. Sergeant
Robert Ring and PC Robert Hydes were on patrol duty, and
they were carrying out a standard check. Ring noted the
number-plate then went off to check it with the computer;
while he radioed, he told PC Hydes to get into the back of
the Rover. Sutcliffe asked if he could get out to urinate and
Hydes gave permission: Sutcliffe stood by an oil storage
tank a few feet away, then got back into the car. Meanwhile,
the sergeant had discovered that the number-plates did not

belong to the Rover, and told Sutcliffe he would have to return to the police station. In the station, Sutcliffe again asked to go to the lavatory and was given permission. It was when the police made him empty his pockets and found a length of clothes-line that they began to suspect that they might have trapped Britain's most wanted man.

To begin with, Sutcliffe lied fluently about why he was carrying the rope and why he was in the car with a prostitute. It was the following day that Sergeant Ring learned about Sutcliffe's brief absence from the car to relieve himself, and went to look near the oil storage tank. In the leaves, he found a ball-headed hammer and a knife. Then he recalled Sutcliffe's trip to the lavatory at the police station. In the cistern he found a second knife. When Sutcliffe was told that he was in serious trouble, he suddenly admitted that he was the Ripper, and confessed to eleven murders. (It seems odd that he got the number wrong – he was later charged with thirteen – but it is possible that he genuinely lost count. He was originally suspected of fourteen murders, but the police later decided that the killing of another prostitute, Jean Harrison – whose body was found in Preston, Lancashire – was not one of the series. She had been raped and the semen was not of Sutcliffe's blood group.)

A card written by Sutcliffe and displayed in his lorry read: "In this truck is a man whose latent genius, if unleashed, would rock the nation, whose dynamic energy would overpower those around him. Better let him sleep?"

The story that began to emerge was of a lonely and shy individual, brooding and introverted, who was morbidly fascinated by prostitutes and red-light areas. He was born on 2 June 1946, the eldest of five children and his mother's favourite. His school career was undistinguished and he left at fifteen. He drifted aimlessly from job to job, including one as a grave-digger in the Bingley cemetery, from which he was dismissed for bad timekeeping. (His later attempt at a defence of insanity rested on a claim that a voice had spoken to him from a cross in the cemetery telling him he had a God-given mission to kill prostitutes.)

In 1967, when he was twenty-one, he met a sixteen-year-old Czech girl, Sonia Szurma, in a pub, and they began going out together. It would be another seven years before they married. The relationship seems to have been stormy; at one point, she was going out with an ice-cream salesman, and Sutcliffe picked up a prostitute "to get even". He was unable to have intercourse, and the woman went off with a £10 note and failed to return with his £5 change. When he saw her in a pub two weeks later and asked for the money, she jeered at him and left him with a sense of helpless fury and humiliation. This, he claimed, was the source of his hatred of prostitutes. In 1969 he made his first attack on a prostitute, hitting her on the head with a sock full of gravel. In October of that year, he was caught carrying a hammer and charged with being equipped for theft; he was fined £25. In 1971 he went for a drive with a friend, Trevor Birdsall, and left the car in the red-light area of Bradford. When he returned ten minutes later he said, "Drive off quickly," and admitted that he had hit a woman with a brick in a sock. Sutcliffe was again driving with Birdsall in 1975 on the evening that Olive Smelt was struck down with a hammer.

In 1972 Sonia Szurma went to London for a teacher's training course and had a nervous breakdown; she was diagnosed as schizophrenic. Two years later, she and Sutcliffe married, but the marriage was punctuated by violent rows — Sutcliffe said he became embarrassed in case the neighbours heard the shouts, implying that it was she who was shouting rather than he. He also told the prostitute Olive Reivers that he had been arguing with his wife "about not being able to go with her", which Olive Reivers took to mean that they were having sexual problems. Certainly, this combination of two introverted people can hardly have improved Sutcliffe's mental condition.

Sutcliffe's first murder – of Wilma McCann – took place in the year after he married Sonia. He admitted: "I developed and played up a hatred for prostitutes . . ." Unlike the Düsseldorf sadist of the 1920s, Peter Kürten, Sutcliffe never admitted to having orgasms as he stabbed his victims; but anyone acquainted with the psychology of sexual criminals would take it for granted that this occurred, and that in most of the cases where the victim was not stabbed, or was left alive, he achieved orgasm at an earlier stage than usual. The parallels are remarkable. Kürten, like Sutcliffe, used a variety of weapons, including a hammer. On one occasion when a corpse remained undiscovered, Kürten also returned to inflict fresh indignities on it. Sutcliffe had returned to the body of Jean Jordan and attempted to cut off the head with a hacksaw.

It was when he pulled up Wilma McCann's clothes and stabbed her in the breast and abdomen that Sutcliffe realized that he had discovered a new sexual thrill. With the second victim, Emily Jackson, he pulled off her bra and briefs, then stabbed her repeatedly – he was, in effect, committing rape with a knife, Sutcliffe was caught in the basic trap of the sex criminal: the realization that he had found a way of inducing a far, more powerful sexual satisfaction than he was able to obtain in normal intercourse, and that he was pushing himself into the position of a social outcast. He admitted sobbing in his car after one of the murders, and being upset to discover that Jayne MacDonald had not been a prostitute (and later, that her father had died of a broken heart). But the compulsion to kill was becoming a fever, so that he no longer cared that the later victims were not prostitutes. He said, probably with sincerity, "The devil drove me."

Sutcliffe's trial began on 5 May 1981. He had pleaded not guilty to murder on grounds of diminished responsibility, and told the story of his "mission" from God. But a warder had overheard him tell his wife that if he could convince the jury that he was mad, he would only spend ten years in a "loony bin". The Attorney-General, Sir Michael Havers, also pointed out that Sutcliffe had at first behaved perfectly normally, laughing at the idea that he might be mentally abnormal, and had introduced the talk of "voices" fairly late in his admissions to the police. On 22 May Sutcliffe was found guilty of murder, and jailed for life, with a recommendation that he should serve at least thirty years.

Dennis Nilsen

On the evening of 8 February 1983, a drains maintenance engineer named Michael Cattran was asked to call at 23 Cranley Gardens, in Muswell Hill, north London, to find out why tenants had been unable to flush their toilets since the previous Saturday. Although Muswell Hill is known as a highly respectable area of London − it was once too expensive for anyone but the upper middle classes − No. 23 proved to be a rather shabby house, divided into flats. A tenant showed Cattran the manhole cover that led to the drainage system. When he removed it, he staggered back and came close to vomiting; the smell was unmistakably decaying flesh. And when he had climbed down the rungs into the cistern, Cattran discovered what was blocking the drain: masses of rotting meat, much of it white, like chicken flesh. Convinced this was human flesh, Cattran rang his supervisor, who decided to come and inspect it in the morning. When they arrived the following day, the drain had been cleared. And a female tenant told them she had heard footsteps going up and down the stairs for much of the night. The footsteps seemed to go up to the top flat, which was rented by a thirty-seven-year-old civil servant named Dennis Nilsen.

Closer search revealed that the drain was still not quite clear; there was a piece of flesh, six inches square, and some bones that resembled fingers. Detective Chief Inspector Peter Jay, of Hornsey CID, was waiting in the hallway of the house that evening when Dennis Nilsen walked in from his day at the office – a Jobcentre in Kentish Town. He told Nilsen he wanted to talk to him about the drains. Nilsen invited the policeman into his flat, and Jay's face wrinkled as he smelt the odour of decaying flesh. He told Nilsen that they had found human remains in the drain, and asked what had happened to the rest of the body. "It's in there, in two plastic bags," said Nilsen, pointing to a wardrobe.

In the police car, the Chief Inspector asked Nilsen whether the remains came from one body or two. Calmly, without emotion, Nilsen said: "There have been fifteen or sixteen altogether."

At the police station, Nilsen – a tall man with metal rimmed glasses – seemed eager to talk. (In fact, he proved to be something of a compulsive talker, and his talk overflowed into a series of school exercise books in which he later wrote his story for the use of Brian Masters, a young writer who contacted him in prison.) He told police that he had murdered three men in the Cranley Gardens house – into which he moved in the autumn of 1981 – and twelve or thirteen at his previous address, 195 Melrose Avenue, Cricklewood.

The plastic bags from the Muswell Hill flat contained two severed heads, and a skull from which the flesh had been stripped – forensic examinaation revealed that it had been boiled. The bathroom contained the whole lower half of a torso, from the waist down, intact. The rest was in bags in the wardrobe and in the tea chest. At Melrose Avenue, thirteen days and nights of digging revealed many human bones, as well as a cheque book and pieces of clothing.

The self-confessed mass murderer – he seemed to take a certain pride in being "Britain's biggest mass murderer" –

was a Scot, born at Fraserburgh on 23 November 1945. His mother, born Betty Whyte, married a Norwegian soldier named Olav Nilsen in 1942. It was not a happy marriage; Olav was seldom at home, and was drunk a great deal; they were divorced seven years after their marriage. In 1954, Mrs Nilsen married again and became Betty Scott. Dennis grew up in the house of his grandmother and grandfather, and was immensely attached to his grandfather, Andrew Whyte, who became a father substitute. When Nilsen was seven, his grandfather died and his mother took Dennis in to see the corpse. This seems to have been a traumatic experience; in his prison notes he declares "My troubles started there." The death of his grandfather was such a blow that it caused his own emotional death, according to Nilsen. Not long after this, someone killed the two pigeons he kept in an air raid shelter, another severe shock. His mother's remarriage when he was nine had the effect of making him even more of a loner.

In 1961, Nilsen enlisted in the army, and became a cook. It was during this period tht he began to get drunk regularly, although he remained a loner, avoiding close relationships. In 1972 he changed the life of a soldier for that of a London policeman, but disliked the relative lack of freedom – compared to the army – and resigned after only eleven months. He became a security guard for a brief period, then a job-interviewer for the Manpower Services Commission.

In November 1975, Nilsen began to share a north London flat – in Melrose Avenue – with a young man named David Gallichan, ten years his junior. Gallichan was later to insist that there was no homosexual relationship, and this is believable. Many heterosexual young men would later accept Nilsen's offer of a bed for the night, and he would make no advances, or accept a simple "No" without resentment. But in May 1977, Gallichan decided he could bear London no longer, and accepted a job in the country. Nilsen was furious; he felt rejected and deserted. The break-up of the relationship with Gallichan — whom he had always dominated — seems to have triggered the homicidal violence that would claim fifteen lives.

The killings began more than a year later, in December 1978. Around Christmas, Nilsen picked up a young Irish labourer in the Cricklewood Arms, and they went back to his flat to continue drinking. Nilsen wanted him to stay over the New Year but the Irishman had other plans. In a note he later wrote for his biographer Brian Masters, Nilsen gives as his motive for this first killing that he was lonely and wanted to spare himself the pain of separation. In another confession he also implies that he has no memory of the actual killing. Nilsen strangled the unnamed Irishman in his sleep with a tie. Then he undressed the body and carefully washed it, a ritual he observed in all his killings. After that, he placed the body under the floorboards where — as incredible as it seems — he kept it until the following August. He eventually burned it on a bonfire at the bottom of the garden, burning some rubber at the same time to cover the smell.

In November 1979, Nilsen attempted to strangle a young Chinaman who had accepted his offer to return to the flat; the Chinaman escaped and reported the attack to the police. But the police believed Nilsen's explanation that the Chinaman was trying to "rip him off" and decided not to pursue the matter.

The next murder victim was a twenty-three-year-old Canadian called Kenneth James Ockendon, who had completed a technical training course and was taking a holiday before starting his career. He had been staying with an uncle and aunt in Carshalton after touring the Lake District. He was not a homosexual, and it was pure bad luck that he got into conversation with Nilsen in the Princess Louise in High Holborn around 3 December 1979. They went back to Nilsen's flat, ate ham, eggs and chips, and bought £20 worth of alcohol. Ockendon watched television, then listened to rock music on Nilsen's hi-fi system. Then he sat listening to music wearing earphones, watching television at the same time. This may have been what cost him his life; Nilsen liked to talk, and probably felt "rejected". "I thought bloody good guest this . . ." And sometime after midnight, while Ockendon was still wearing the headphones, he strangled him with a flex. Ockendon was so drunk that he put up no struggle. And Nilsen was also so drunk that after the murder, he sat down, put on the headphones, and went on playing music for hours. When he tried to put the body under the floorboards the next day, rigor mortis had set in and it was impossible. He had to wait until the rigor had passed. Later, he dissected the body. Ockendon had large quantities of Canadian money in his moneybelt, but Nilsen tore this up. The rigorous Scottish upbringing would not have allowed him to steal.

Nilsen's accounts of the murders are repetitive, and make them sound mechanical and almost identical. The third victim in May 1980, was a sixteen-year-old butcher named Martyn Duffey, who was also strangled and placed under the floorboards. Number four was a twenty-six-year-old Scot named Billy Sutherland — again strangled in his sleep with a tie and placed under the floorboards. Number five was an unnamed Mexican or Philipino, killed a few months later. Number six was an Irish building worker. Number seven was an undernourished down-and-out picked up in a doorway. (He was burned on the bonfire all in one piece.) The next five victims, all unnamed, were killed equally casually between late 1980 and late 1981. Nilsen later insisted that all the murders had been without sexual motivation — a plea that led Brian Masters to entitle his book on the case *Killing for Company*. There are moments in Nilsen's confessions when it sounds as if, like so many serial killers, he felt as if he was being taken over by a Mr Hyde personality or possessed by some demonic force.

In October 1981, Nilsen moved into an upstairs flat in Cranley Gardens, Muswell Hill. On 25 November, he took a homosexual student named Paul Nobbs back with him, and they got drunk. The next day, Nobbs went into University College Hospital for a check-up, and was told that bruises on his throat indicated that someone had tried to strangle him. Nilsen apparently changed his mind at the last moment.

The next victim, John Howlett, was less lucky. He woke up as Nilsen tried to strangle him and fought back hard; Nilsen had to bang his head against the headrest of the bed to subdue him. When he realized Howlett was still breathing, Nilsen drowned him in the bath. He hacked up the body in the bath, then boiled chunks in a large pot to make them easier to dispose of. (He also left parts of the body out in plastic bags for the dustbin men to take away.)

In May 1982, another intended victim escaped — a drag-artiste called Carl Stottor. After trying to strangle him, Nilsen placed him in a bath of water, but changed his mind and allowed him to live. When he left the flat, Stottor even agreed to meet Nilsen again — but decided not to keep the appointment. He decided not to go to the police.

The last two victims were both unnamed, one a drunk and one a drug-addict. In both cases, Nilsen claims to be unable to remember the actual killing. Both were dissected, boiled and flushed down the toilet. It was after this second murder — the fifteenth in all — that the tenants complained about blocked drains, and Nilsen was arrested.

The trial began on 24 October 1983, in the same court where Peter Sutcliffe had been tried two years earlier. Nilsen was charged with six murders and two attempted murders, although he had confessed to fifteen murders and seven attempted murders. He gave the impression that he was enjoying his moment of glory. The defence pleaded diminished responsibility, and argued that the charge should be reduced to manslaughter. The jury declined to accept this, and on 4 November 1983, Nilsen was found guilty by a vote of 10 to 2, and sentenced to life imprisonment.

Richard Ramirez

Throughout 1985 handgun sales in Los Angeles soared. Many suburbanites slept with a loaded pistol by their beds. A series of violent attacks upon citizens in their own homes had shattered the comfortably normality of middle class life. Formerly safe neighbourhoods seemed to be the killer's favourite targets. The whole city was terrified.

The attacks were unprecedented in many ways. Neither murder nor robbery seemed to be the obvious motive, although both frequently took place. The killer would break into a house, creep into the main bedroom and shoot the male partner through the head with a .22. He would then rape and beat the wife or girlfriend, suppressing resistance with threats of violence to her or her children. Male children were sometimes sodomized, the rape victims sometimes shot. On occasion, he would ransack the house looking for valuables while at other times he would leave empty-handed without searching. During the attacks he would force victims to declare their love for Satan. Survivors described a tall, slim Hispanic male with black, greasy hair and severely decayed teeth. The pattern of crimes seemed to be based less upon a need to murder or rape but a desire to terrify and render helpless. More than most serial killers the motive seemed to be exercising power.

The killer also had unusual methods of victim selection. He seemed to be murdering outside his own racial group, preferring Caucasians and specifically Asians. He also seemed to prefer to break into yellow houses.

In the spring and summer of 1985 there were more than twenty attacks, most of which involved both rape and murder. By the end of March the press had picked up the pattern and splashed stories connecting the series of crimes. After several abortive nicknames, such as "The Walk-In Killer" or "The Valley Invader", the *Herald Examiner* came up with "The Night Stalker", a name sensational enough to stick.

Thus all through the hot summer of 1985 Californians slept with their windows closed. One policeman commented to a reporter: "People are armed and staying up late. Burglars want this guy caught like everyone else. He's making it bad for their business." The police themselves circulated sketches and stopped anyone who looked remotely like The Night Stalker. One innocent man was stopped five times.

Despite these efforts and thorough forensic analysis of crime scenes there was little progress in the search for the killer's identity.

Things were obviously getting difficult for The Night Stalker as well. The next murder that fitted the pattern occurred in San Francisco, showing perhaps that public awareness in Los Angeles had made it too taxing a location. This shift also gave police a chance to search San Francisco hotels for records of a man of The Night Stalker's description. Sure enough, while checking the downmarket Tenderloin district, police learned that a thin Hispanic with bad teeth had been staying at a cheap hotel there periodically over the past year. On the last occasion he had checked out the night of the San Francisco attack. The manager commented that his room "smelled like a skunk" each time he vacated it and it took three days for the smell to clear.

Though this evidence merely confirmed the police's earlier description, The Night Stalker's next shift of location was to prove more revealing. A young couple in

Mission Viejo were attacked in their home. The Night Stalker shot the man through the head while he slept, then raped his partner on the bed next to the body. He then tied her up while he ransacked the house for money and jewellery. Before leaving he raped her a second time and force her to fellate him with a gun pressed against her head. Unfortunately for the killer, however, his victim caught a glimpse of him escaping in a battered orange Toyota and memorized the license plate. She immediately alerted the police. LAPD files showed that the car had been stolen in Los Angeles' Chinatown district while the owner was eating in a restaurant. An all-points bulletin was put out for the vehicle, and officers were instructed not to try and arrest the driver, merely to observe him. However, the car was not found. In fact, The Night Stalker had dumped the car soon after the attack, and it was located two days later in a car park in Los Angeles' Rampart district. After plain clothes officers had kept the car under surveillance for twenty-four hours, the police moved in and took the car away for forensic testing. A set of fingerprints was successfully lifted.

Searching police fingerprint files for a match manually can take many days and even then it is possible to miss correlations. However, the Los Angeles police had recently installed a fingerprint database computer system, designed by the FBI, and it was through this that they checked the set of fingerprints from the orange Toyota. The system works by storing information about the relative distance between different features of a print, and comparing them with a digitized image of the suspect's fingerprint. The search provided a positive match and a photograph. The Night Stalker was a petty thief and burglar. His name was Ricardo Leyva Ramirez.

The positive identification was described by the forensic division as "a near miracle". The computer system had only just been installed, this was one of its first trials. Furthermore, the system only contained the fingerprints of criminals born after 1 January, 1960. Richard Ramirez was born in February 1960.

The police circulated the photograph to newspapers, and it was shown on the late evening news. At the time, Ramirez was in Phoenix, buying cocaine with the money he had stolen in Mission Viejo. On the morning that the papers splashed his name and photograph all over their front pages, he was on a bus on the way back to Los Angeles, unaware that he had been identified.

He arrived safely and went into the bus station toilet to finish off the cocaine he had bought. No one seemed to be overly interested in him as he left the station and walked through Los Angeles. Ramirez was a Satanist, and had developed a belief that Satan himself watched over him, preventing his capture.

At 8.15 a.m. Ramirez entered Tito's Liquor Store at 819 Towne Avenue. He selected some Pepsi and a pack of sugared doughnuts; he had a sweet tooth that, coupled with a lack of personal hygiene, had left his mouth with only a few blackened teeth. At the counter other customers looked at him strangely as he produced three dollar bills and awaited his change. Suddenly he noticed the papers' front pages, and his faith in Satan's power must have been shaken. He dodged out of the shop and ran, accompanied by shouts of, "It is him! Call the cops!" He pounded off down the street at a surprising speed for one so ostensibly unhealthy. Within twelve minutes he had covered two miles. He had headed east. He was in the Hispanic district of Los Angeles.

Ever since the police had confirmed that The Night Stalker was Hispanic there had been a great deal of anger among the Hispanic community of Los Angeles. They felt that racial stereotypes were already against them enough without their being associated with psychopaths. Thus more than most groups, Hispanics wanted The Night Stalker out of action.

Cults and Fanatics

Ramirez, by now, was desperate to get a vehicle. He attempted to pull a woman from her car in a supermarket lot until he was chased away by some customers of the barber's shop opposite. He carried on running, though exhausted, into the more residential areas of east Los Angeles. There, he tried to steal a 1966 red mustang having failed to notice that the owner, Faustino Pinon was lying underneath repairing it. As Ramirez attempted to start the car Pinon grabbed him by the collar and tried to pull him from the driver's seat. Ramirez shouted that he had a gun, but Pinon carried on pulling at him even after the car had started, causing it to career into the gatepost. Ramirez slammed it into reverse and accelerated into the side of Pinon's garage, and the vehicle stalled. Pinon succeeded in wrenching Ramirez out of his car, but in the following struggle Ramirez escaped, leaping the fence and running off across the road. There he tried to wrestle Angelina De La Torres from her Ford Granada. "Te voy a matar! (I'm going to kill you!)" screamed Ramirez, "Give me the keys!", but again he was thwarted and he ran away, now pursued by a growing crowd of neighbours. Manuel De La Torres, Angelina's husband succeeded in smashing Ramirez on the head with a gate bar and he fell, but he managed to struggle up and set off running again before he could be restrained. Incredibly, when Ramirez had developed a lead, he stopped, turned around and stuck his tongue out at his pursuers, then sped off once more. His stamina could not hold indefinitely however, and it was De La Torres who again tackled him and held him down. It is possible that Ramirez would have been lynched there and then had not a patrolman called to the scene arrived. Coincidentally the patrolman was the same age as the killer, and he too was called Ramirez. He reached the scene just as The Night Stalker disappeared under the mob. He drove his patrol car to within a few feet of where Ramirez was restrained, got out and prepared to handcuff the captive.

"Save me. Please. Thank God you're here. It's me, I'm the one you want. Save me before they kill me," babbled Ramirez. The patrolman handcuffed him and pushed him into the back of the car. The crowd was becoming restless, and the car was kicked as it pulled away. Sixteen-year-old Felipe Castaneda, part of the mob that captured Ramirez remarked, "He should never, *never* have come to East LA. He might have been a tough guy, but he came to a tough neighbourhood. He was Hispanic. He should have known better."

"The Night Stalker" was in custody, at first in a police holding cell and then in Los Angeles county jail. While in police care he repeatedly admitted to being "The Night Stalker" and begged to be killed.

The case against Ramirez was strong. The murder weapon, a .22 semi-automatic pistol was found in the possession of a woman in Tijuana, who had been given it by a friend of Ramirez. Police also tried to track down some of the jewellery that Ramirez had stolen and fenced, by sending investigators to his birth-place El Paso, a spiralling town on the Texas-Mexico border. Questioning his family and neighbours revealed that Ramirez' early life had been spent in petty theft and smoking a lot of marijuana. He had never joined any of the rival teenage gangs that fight over territory throughout El Paso, preferring drugs and listening to Heavy Metal. It had been common knowledge that Ramirez was a Satanist; a boyhood friend, Tom Ramos said he believed that it was Bible-study classes that had turned the killer that way.

The investigators also found a great deal of jewellery, stashed at the house of Ramirez' sister Rosa Flores. The police were also hoping to find a pair of eyes that Ramirez had gouged from one of his victims that had not been found in any previous searches. Unfortunately they were not recovered.

The evidence against Ramirez now seemed unequivocal. In a controversial move, the Mayor of Los Angeles said that whatever went on in court, he was convinced of Ramirez' guilt. This was later to prove a mainstay in a defence argument that Ramirez could not receive a fair trial in Los Angeles.

The appointed chief prosecutor in the case was deputy District Attorney P. Philip Halpin, who had prosecuted the "Onion Field" cop-killing case twenty years earlier. Halpin hoped to end the trial and have Ramirez in the gas chamber in a relatively short period of time. The prosecutor drew up a set of initial charges and submitted them as quickly as possible. A public defender was appointed to represent Ramirez. However Ramirez' family had engaged an El Paso lawyer, Manuel Barraza, and Ramirez eventually rejected his appointed public defender in favour of the El Paso attorney. Barraza did not even have a license to practise law in California.

Ramirez accepted, then rejected three more lawyers, finally settling upon two defenders, Dan and Arturo Hernandez. The two were not related, although they often worked together. The judge advised Ramirez that his lawyers did not even meet the minimum requirements for trying a death-penalty case in California, but Ramirez insisted, and more than seven weeks after the initial charges were filed, pleas of Not Guilty were entered on all counts.

The Hernandez' and Ramirez seemed to be trying to force Halpin into making a mistake out of sheer frustration, and thus to create a mis-trial. After each hearing the Hernandez' made pleas for, and obtained, more time to prepare their case. Meanwhile one prosecution witness had died of natural causes, and Ramirez' appearance was gradually changing. He had had his hair permed, and his rotten teeth replaced. This naturally introduced more uncertainty into the minds of prosecution witnesses as to Ramirez identity. The racial make-up of the jury was contested by the defence, which caused delays. The defence also argued, with some justification, that Ramirez could not receive a fair trial in Los Angeles, and moved for a change of location. Although the motion was refused it caused yet more delays. It actually took three and a half years for Ramirez' trial to finally get underway.

Halpin's case was, in practical terms, unbeatable. The defence's only real possibility of success was in infinite delay. For the first three weeks of the trial events progressed relatively smoothly. Then Daniel Hernandez announced that the trial would have to be postponed as he was suffering from nervous exhaustion. He had a doctor's report that advised six weeks rest with psychological counselling. It seemed likely that a mis-trial would be declared. Halpin tried to argue that Arturo Hernandez could maintain the defence, even though he had failed to turn up at the hearings and trial for the first seven months. However this proved unnecessary as the judge made a surprise decision and denied Daniel Hernandez his time off, arguing that he had failed to prove a genuine need.

Halpin, by this stage was actually providing the Hernandez' with all the information that they required to mount an adequate defence, in order to move things along and prevent mis-trial. For the same reasons the judge eventually appointed a defence co-counsel, Ray Clark. Clark immediately put the defence on a new track: Ramirez was the victim of a mistaken identity. He even developed an acronym for this defence – SODDI or Some Other Dude Did It. When the defence case opened, Clark produced testimony from Ramirez' father that he had been in El Paso at the time of one of the murders of which he was accused. He also criticized the prosecution for managing to prove that footprints at one of the crime scenes were made by a size eleven-and-a-half Avia trainer, without ever proving that Ramirez actually owned such a shoe. When the jury finally left to deliberate however, it seemed clear that they would find Ramirez guilty.

Things were not quite that easy however. After thirteen days of deliberation, juror Robert Lee was dismissed for inattention and replaced by an alternative who had also witnessed the case. Two days later, juror Phyllis Singletary was murdered in a domestic dispute. Her live-in lover had beaten her then shot her several times. She was also replaced.

At last on 20 September, 1989 after twenty-two days of deliberation the jury returned a verdict of guilty on all thirteen counts of murder, twelve of those in the first degree. The jury also found Ramirez guilty of thirty other felonies, including burglary, rape, sodomy and attempted murder. Asked by reporters how he felt after the verdict, Ramirez replied, "Evil".

There remained only the selection of sentence. At the hearing Clark argued that Ramirez might actually have been possessed by the devil, or that alternatively he had been driven to murder by over-active hormones. He begged the jury to imprison Ramirez for life rather than put him on death row. If the jury agreed, Clark pointed out, "he will never see Disneyland again," surely punishment enough. After five further days of deliberation, the jury voted for the death penalty. Again, reporters asked Ramirez how he felt about the outcome as he was being taken away, "Big deal. Death always went with the territory. I'll see you in Disneyland."

Any attempt to trace the source of Ramirez' violent behaviour runs up against an insurmountable problem. No external traumas or difficulties seem to have brutalized him. He had a poor upbringing, he was part of a racial minority, but these things alone cannot explain such an incredibly sociopathic personality. Ramirez seems to have created himself. He was an intelligent and deeply religious child. Having decided at some stage that counter-culture and drug-taking provided a more appealing lifestyle, he developed pride in his separateness. In the El Paso of his early manhood, people would lock their doors if they saw him coming down the street. He was known as "Ricky Rabon", Ricky the thief, a nickname he enjoyed as he felt it made him "someone". By the time he moved to Los Angeles, he was injecting cocaine and probably committing burglaries to support himself. He let his teeth rot away, eating only childish sugary foods. He refused to wash. He listened to loud Heavy Metal music.

It has been argued that it was his taste in music that drove him to murder and Satanism, but this would seem to be more part of the mood of censorship sweeping America than a genuine explanation. Anyone who takes the trouble to listen to the music in question, particularly the AC/DC album cited by American newspapers at the time of the murders, will find that there is little in it to incite violence.

Ramirez' obvious attempts to repel others in his personal behaviour, and his heavy drug use seem more likely sources of violence than early poverty or music. His assumed "otherness" seems in retrospect sadly underdeveloped, having never progressed beyond a teenager's need to appal staid grown-up society.

This is not to say that Ramirez was unintelligent. His delaying of his trial and his choice of the Hernandez' to continue the delays, shows that he had worked out the most effective method of staying alive for the longest period either before, or soon after he was captured. His remarks in court upon being sentenced were not particularly original, yet they are articulate:

"It's nothing you'd understand but I do have something to say . . . I don't believe in the hypocritical, moralistic dogma of this so-called civilized society. I need not look beyond this room to see all the liars, haters, the killers, the crooks, the paranoid cowards — truly *trematodes* of the Earth, each one in his own legal profession. You maggots make me sick — hypocrites one and all . . . I am beyond your experience. I am beyond good and evil, legions of the night, night breed, repeat not the errors of the Night Prowler [a name from an AC/DC song] and show no mercy. I will be avenged. Lucifer dwells within us all. That's it."

Ramirez remains on death row. It is unlikely that he will be executed before the year 2000.

Titles in the World Famous series

World Famous Cults and Fanatics

World Famous Scandals

World Famous Strange Tales and Weird Mysteries

World Famous Crimes of Passion

World Famous Unsolved Crimes

World Famous Catastrophes